The Last Laugh

D1564530

FOLKLORE STUDIES
IN A MULTICULTURAL
WORLD

The Folklore Studies in a Multicultural World series is a collaborative venture of the University of Illinois Press, the University Press of Mississippi, the University of Wisconsin Press, and the American Folklore Society, made possible by a generous grant from the Andrew W. Mellon Foundation. The series emphasizes the interdisciplinary and international nature of current folklore scholarship, documenting connections between communities and their cultural production. Series volumes highlight aspects of folklore studies such as world folk cultures, folk art and music, foodways, dance, African American and ethnic studies, gender and queer studies, and popular culture.

The Last Laugh

FOLK HUMOR, CELEBRITY CULTURE, AND
MASS-MEDIATED DISASTERS IN THE DIGITAL AGE

Trevor J. Blank

THE UNIVERSITY OF WISCONSIN PRESS

The University of Wisconsin Press
1930 Monroe Street, 3rd Floor
Madison, Wisconsin 53711-2059
uwpress.wisc.edu

3 Henrietta Street
London WC2E 8LU, England
eurospanbookstore.com

Printed in the United States of America

Library of Congress Cataloging-in-Publication Data

Blank, Trevor J.
The last laugh : folk humor, celebrity culture, and mass-mediated disasters in the
digital age / Trevor J. Blank.
p.   cm. — (Folklore studies in a multicultural world)
Includes bibliographical references and index.
ISBN 978-0-299-29204-1 (pbk. : alk. paper) — ISBN 978-0-299-29203-4 (e-book)
1. Folklore and the Internet. I. Title. II. Series: Folklore studies in a
multicultural world.
GR44.E43B53   2013
398'.36—dc23
2012032669

To
SIMON J. BRONNER,
the best teacher I've ever had

Contents

Illustrations

Preface

This book aims to demonstrate that the global reach of new media, particularly the Internet, has now irrevocably extended itself into the ways that modern society expresses itself. To illustrate this, I examine the evolution of the humorous visual and especially narrative folk responses to death, disaster, and scandal as they have emerged in technologically mediated expressive communications over time. In doing so, I contend that as a locus of vernacular (or indigenous, unofficial "folk") expression, the allure of the Internet comes from its widespread accessibility and its ability to digitally compensate for individuals' physical detachment within the physical world by providing a unique combination of instantaneity, simultaneity, and heterogeneity. The research presented herein is not intended as a mere survey. I offer a series of case studies that show the explanatory potential of using folkloristic tools to analyze expressive responses to death, disaster, and scandal. Principally, I hope to draw attention to the significant ways in which folk and mass culture have evolved throughout the twentieth and twenty-first centuries and to demonstrate the importance of technologically mediated communication devices for self-expression, especially through the circulation of humorous rhetoric and artistic creations online.

The central point remains that we "are moving away from a world in which some produce and many consume media toward one in which everyone has a more active stake in the culture that is produced" (Jenkins et al. 2009, 12). When collectively observed, the technologically influenced cultural patterns constitute the presence of a significant historical time: the digital age. The distinctiveness of this era became increasingly obvious to pundits who witnessed the progressive sophistication and miniaturization of the personal computer and other broadcasting technologies throughout the 1970s and 1980s (see Ceruzzi

2003; Hafner and Lyon 1998; Ornstein 2002; Ryan 2010). The clunky analog machines that once took up entire rooms have given way to the laptops, tablets, and cellular phones of today that are capable of limitless communicative possibilities. But en route to realizing this pocket-sized digital age, no technological medium has been more influential on human interactivity than the World Wide Web, which almost single-handedly facilitated the assimilation of computer-mediated technology into the daily lives of most Americans by the early 2000s.

Amazingly (or so it now seems), the Internet was not originally designed to serve as a vast digital forum for vernacular expression and social networking but rather to accommodate the research and communication needs of scientists, academics, and military personnel. The development of the technological interfaces that would ultimately lead to the emergence of the digital age began during the Cold War under the U.S. Department of Defense's Advanced Research Projects Agency Network (ARPANET) program, which was created in direct response to the Soviet Union's launching of Sputnik. Beginning in 1958, ARPANET served the military and academic researchers as a means of communication and as a command tool for defense operations. E-mail technology was created in 1970, and by the 1980s people were interacting online through bulletin boards (discussion groups), MUDs (multiuser dungeons), and the WELL (Whole Earth 'Lectronic Link), a social network composed of Internet users from across the globe; later, Internet Relay Chat (IRC) followed (Hafner 2001; Hafner and Lyon 1998; Rheingold 2000). In 1989 English computer scientist Timothy Berners-Lee developed HyperText Markup Language (HTML), which operated web-browsing programs that would eventually allow the Internet to expand from a primarily academic and militaristic forum into the worldwide phenomenon it is today, with limitless boundaries for information retrieval and vernacular expression. Indeed, the very character of the Internet has thematically evolved from being a closed and exclusive venue to an open and democratic place where symbolic interaction flourishes.

The widespread adoption and continued improvement of computer-mediated technologies into the present has had far-reaching effects on the ways that many people now interact with peers on a day-to-day basis. The digital age forges on today; its main identifying feature can be found in Americans' perpetual reliance on computer technology for organizing and informing their lives. Just as the industrial age fundamentally redefined American life and the ways that people went about engaging their society, the digital age has also ushered in tremendous changes in the ways that people conceptualize the life course, human interaction, and self-reliance—primarily through the adoption of simulative venues for symbolic interaction that frequently mask the social contexts and prerogatives of participants.

Outside of social networking sites and online community gatherings that prize personal sharing and actively attempt to replicate the social mechanics of face-to-face decorum, the constructs of race, ethnicity, gender, age, and appearance are ambiguous. The seemingly democratic presentation and inborn autonomy of the Internet suggests an expansion of social groups and looser restrictions to their entry. Many people use the Internet to vibrantly and proudly express themselves through folk art or by posting to discussion forums with a screen name or "handle" that conveys their personality and/or interests (see Aldred 2010; Booth 2008; Foote 2007; Stallabrass 2003). So while the proverb "seeing is believing" may be important to the social categorizations of oral traditions and other folklore from face-to-face contexts, it is far less important on the Internet.

Relationships forged in interactive environments online are not always one-sided or impersonal. On the contrary, as Barbara Warnick notes, rhetoric "functions as ubiquitously on the World Wide Web as it does in other communication environments" (2007, 121). In deep-rooted digital communities, people come to know each other through the established rapport between each other's input to the online dialogue and efforts toward group cohesion. Above all, these interactions are defined by the active *sharing* between participants through symbolic gestures encoded with narratives, visual contributions, or other expressive rhetoric.

Without question, the emergence of the World Wide Web in the 1990s created the need for social and cultural adaptations to the unfamiliar nuances of digitized, computer-mediated communications. However, as evidenced by the hiccups seen during the integrations of radio, television, and cinematic media outlets throughout the twentieth century, such a challenge was to be expected. When times change and the "old time way of life" appears to fade, people engage the dominant culture and make their own modifications to corporate or other outsider influences in their lives en route to producing a new, hybridized vernacular that engages the multifaceted contexts of an individual's creative expression or engagement with society (see Bronner 2004, 2009; Danet 2001; Dégh 1994; Jenkins 2008; P. Smith 1991). Of course, there have been and there always will be those who resist change, just as there are people today who prefer playing checkers in a public space over checking their e-mail in cyberspace.

The "voice of the people"—the folk—is represented today by the merger of two distinct expressive venues: one based in the physical world, the other in a digital one. Where there were once separate mediums that produced specific media content, now both analog and digital venues can interchangeably share content in similar forms. The merging of formerly oral and/or visual means of transmission with digital interface is called "media convergence," and it is a pervasive characteristic of how information is shared and organized in the digital age. Communications scholar Henry Jenkins (2008) has shown that new media and other accompanying, increasingly sophisticated technologies are not simply replacing old forms of media but are also developing a newfangled means of interacting with them altogether in what he calls a "convergence culture." This convergence culture, Jenkins holds, is not simply a technological revolution but is the marker of a cultural shift as well—one that is dependent on participatory culture to maintain the cohesiveness of community and perceived social harmony. In the process of juxtaposing folk culture (the everyday life of localized, tradition-bound groups) within mass society, there is often conflict in ascertaining authenticity and the appropriate folk correlations and derivations that constitute its place in the historical context (Bronner 2004; see also Bendix 1997).

The instant gratification from feeling part of a greater, widespread phenomenon allows users to alleviate their anxieties directly and in ways that they may not be able to in the physical world. Furthermore, the accessibility of the Internet allows for greater participation from widespread demographic groups and beckons users to offer more authentic representations of their sentiments or frustrations about analog media discourses. At the heart of the response to media-induced anxieties is the recitation and sharing of *folklore*—but what exactly is that, and why does it matter?

Many people incorrectly conceptualize folklore as mere fairy tales, old wives' gossip, or urban legends. While it is true that these genres are examples of folklore, their popularity often obscures what the term actually represents. In essence, folklore is the traditional knowledge of individuals and/or their community that is acquired through oral, print, or mediated communication. What makes something "traditional" is not its origin or the influence of time but rather continuities and consistencies that allow a person or group to perceive expressions *as* traditional, locally derived, or community generated (Howard 2008a, 201; see also Georges and Jones 1995).

The word "folklore" is derived from the German *Volkskunde* or "knowledge of the folk." It is a compound of two words: "folk" for people, and "lore" for the inherited or cultural knowledge that they have acquired from tradition. The "folk" have been defined by the late scholar Alan Dundes as "*any group whatsoever* who share at least one common factor" in any social grouping

(Dundes 1980, 6–7, emphasis in original). Usually the linking factor is shared between two or more individuals (Oring 1984a) but can also be composed of a single individual through "solo" folklore as well (see Mechling 2006). Of course, Dundes's original definition of "folk" was conceived with face-to-face interaction in mind. Yet today's new media devices allow for people to digitally consort online with the same expressive range that they would in person. So while our understanding of the "folk" and their culture remains mostly intact, the general consensus about what actually constitutes "folklore" has been undergoing revision and reinterpretation for some time.

Folklore studies from the Brothers Grimm in the early nineteenth century and new scholars in the twentieth century emphasized oral transmission (often by nonliterate persons) of expressive speech as the content of folklore. Noteworthy folklorist William Wells Newell believed that "technology, specifically print, produces the social distinction between high and low that generates folklore" and further concluded that "genuine" folklore was that which escaped print (Newell 1883, v). These views were carried for over a half century by scholars until Richard Dorson (1970) sought to update the definition of folklore for what he called "the modern world" and other enterprising folklorists, like Alan Dundes and Carl Pagter, published a series of popular books on photocopied humor of "urban folklore from the paperwork empire" in which they argued against a definition based on oral transmission or the absence of technology (Dundes and Pagter [1975] 1978, 1989, 1991b, 1996, 2000). As some scholars graciously or reluctantly accepted these inclusions, newer technologies became widely adopted by ordinary people. Nevertheless, many folklorists remain skeptical.

The presence of technology does *not* diminish the validity of folkloric materials. Over time, fax machines, photocopiers, and eventually primitive e-mail and "bulletin board" discussion lists all managed to lay the groundwork for many of the folkloric expressive forms that we see online today (see Michael 1995; Preston 1994; Roemer 1994). For example, the rhetorical motifs found in the "pre-Internet" circulation of technologically mediated folklore such as "Xerox humor" (once a mainstay of communal workspaces) resurfaced in the form of forwarded chain e-mails that similarly circulate without the knowledge of the originating authorial source and frequently contain manipulated pictures, cheeky folk wisdom, or urban legends. So folklore is not necessarily a study of the past (or cultural "survivals") but is rather the study of traditional beliefs and practices, conventional knowledge, and expressive patterns as they surface in contemporary society. How these traditions are received and subsequently change or remain the same over time is of central concern to folklorists, and the study of this phenomenon also includes a consideration of historical contexts and how they served to shape and mediate the passing of tradition (see Bronner 1998, 2000, 2002).

If folklore can be conceptually defined by its transmission, it can be defined operationally by its pattern of repetition and variation (also called "multiple variation"), a key concept for explaining changes observed in patterns of folkloric expression over time. In essence, repetition and variation refers to multiple existences and replications of folkloric materials across space and time. After all, as folklore disseminates it is repeated, revised, and reinterpreted before shifting into new contexts where it obtains new meaning among new actors, which regularly leads to multiple variations of a single text (Dégh and Vázsonyi 1975; see also Dundes 1999).

All ideas, symbolic interactions, and expressive behaviors must go through a social and communicative process by which they are conceived, interpreted, and subsequently repeated and/or varied (see Levine 1988, 33). This may be distinguished as a *folk process* because it is a learned expressive behavioral pattern that has been honed over generations in order to establish social conventions for knowledge sharing and the encoding of contextual values assigned within a particular community. More explicitly, the folk process can be classified as the means by which individuals and/or their community interprets and reacts to information accrual in the course of advancing their social progression or education. *Folkloristics* is the academic study of folklore in a variety of social, cultural, and other performative or expressive contexts (Georges and Jones 1995).[1]

Like folklore, *humor* is not simply a genre but rather a theme of material considered to be "funny" or amusing within the context or performance in which it is transmitted to an audience. Typically, notes sociologist Christie Davies, "Those at whom we are laughing are behaving in ways that are incongruous and which break the social conventions that prohibit and exclude such foolishness in speech and behavior but in a context that we know is fictitious and harmless" (2011, 20). That is, humor is not usually created out of hostility but, rather, for playful and often self-deprecating purposes (see Davies 2002, 2011). Humor can take the form of jokes, anecdotes, riddles, gesturing, comics, narrative comedy, wordplay, witty rhetoric, or silly artwork, just to name a few types. Again, the context of transmission may influence the materials' reception. "Flipping the bird" to someone may convey directed anger, but it can also be used to playfully rebuff a peer's teasing in the course of a conversation; this speaks to the fact that the dynamics of humor may vary across face-to-face and online contexts. However, in both venues the sharing or performance of humor often enables individuals to rhetorically test their own compatibility with peers.

Many forms of humor can be categorized as predominantly sexual and aggressive in their intentions, although this is not necessarily a given. According to Sigmund Freud, humor allows people to "evade restrictions and open sources of pleasure that have become inaccessible" because of repression, social constraints, or contextual circumstances (1905, 103; see also Dundes 1987b; Oring 1984b). Drawing off the cues of incongruities that may emerge, humor affords people the freedom to express sentiments and thoughts that may otherwise be considered socially reprehensible in a playful, harmless way. Thus, jokesters bypass or dismiss expected conventions of "appropriate behavior" by rhetorically rejecting the seriousness of occasions that would typically be considered disheartening. As Hungarian ethnologist Lajos Csaszi notes: "Catastrophe jokes can be regarded as forms of ritual communication not only because of the cyclical nature of their dissemination and the formalized nature of their reception but also because of their characteristic contents. They do not simply reflect events, but rather they consciously offend against norms and symbolically reverse those rules that under normal circumstances determine how one is to speak of the catastrophe" (2003, 185). Indeed, disaster jokes are a "rebellion against the official discourse about humor: that humor is inappropriate in times of disaster and that some topics are too serious to be joked about" (Kuipers 2011, 43). One of the primary reasons for joking about morbid topics such as disasters, tragedies, or death is the desire to "speak the last word" about unspeakable events, often in rhetorical opposition to the inescapable, repetitive narratives espoused by media outlets (Ellis 2001, 8). As Christie Davies explains, "The flourishing of jokes about *specific shocking events* in the last thirty years or so *is a product* of the rise of mass media and of the direct, dogmatic and yet ambiguous and paradoxical way in which accidents and disasters are presented to the public by the media" (1999, 255, emphasis in original). Consequently, the "*global* television reporting of distant disasters has led to jokes that place these events within a framework of *local* trivia" (Davies 2003, 21, emphasis in original). The Internet venue affords users the freedom to counter such hegemonic reportage tactics without the looming threat of physical confrontation or fear of damaging their "real world" reputations if they speak out. The robust commentarial discourse online is a safe place for users to engage or experiment in a dialogue with other like-minded individuals; or, conversely, users may vivaciously spar with one another in a playfully aggressive and instigative manner. Humor is a major tool within Internet users' expressive arsenal.

Mobile communications—not just the World Wide Web in wireless form but also text messaging, streaming newsfeeds, and cell phones—symbolize the modern connection to society. People still line up for hours (and sometimes even days) awaiting the release of a new iPhone or video game system in the hopes of being among the first to consume the latest and greatest. Is the motivation to buy new techie gear charged with the desire to achieve symbolic status in one's social network, or is it more basic than this? Could it be that the true motivation lies within the individual and their desire to connect to others in the most efficient and sexy way possible? The material culture of the technological object surely serves as a projection of one's desired presentation of self, but the *use* of the medium is characterized by the individual's interaction with others. At the end of the day, consumption only goes so far—devices must serve a purpose or lose their relevancy. In actuality, the dynamics of the expressive mediums are the main attraction.

Computer-mediated communication in the digital age boasts such far-reaching influence by perpetually enhancing the interfacial aspects most cherished by users, chiefly speed (instantaneity), connection (simultaneity), and choice (heterogeneity). From a tradition-centered and historical perspective, these desirable traits can be traced to the emergent attitudes about the technology that surfaced after World War II (Lowe 1983; see also Bronner 1986). Nevertheless, new devices that stretch the limits of functionality *do* carry aesthetic value as material objects, while also possessing social power through semiotic transference of the individual's symbolic connectedness with the surrounding world. Actually utilizing appropriate technological devices en route to a greater digital experience is the ultimate prize.

The mainstream support for greater speed, connectivity, and choice among Internet users has culminated in a registry of values about what communicative technological devices should and should not be—including how they should be engaged by individuals while in use. When adopted, these dominant attitudes and expectations of the digital experience reflect the social construction of a digitized *folk system*—a cultural domain that is regulated by the common practices and reinforced behavioral expectations as determined, modeled, and accepted by the people who make up the Internet community's constituency themselves. These folk systems provide a semblance of social belonging but, more important, convey a sense of tradition within modernity.

The user-facilitated dynamics of folk systems may contribute toward a *folk web*—online participatory media that is regulated by amateur users (such as discussion forums and blogs). As a result of the digital folk system and its ability to model behavioral expectations therein, the unwritten philosophies of Internet folklore grow to dictate online decorum (or "Netiquette," as earlier Internet users called it) and influence how one should best participate or navigate the consummation of relationships online, either generally or in the context of a single site or a web-based community. The governing rules will vary between competing social groups that have organized online.

With a clearer picture of folklore in place, I hope that the prevalent theoretical orientation from which I derive my analysis is more transparent. However, before my research and analysis can be most efficiently presented in the ensuing chapters of this work, there are several other crucial terms, concepts, and methodologies that merit explanation in order to properly inform the context of this research and provide insight into my rationale for undertaking this project in the first place. The first terms that I wish to explain are *digital natives* and *digital immigrants*.

In 2001 educator Marc Prensky coined the term "digital native" to conceptualize those individuals who were born after 1980 and thus had been inherently subjected to the social influences of burgeoning communicative technologies throughout their lives (Prensky 2001a, 2001b). In essence, these "native" individuals have never known a world in which technology, broadly construed, has not been a major source of entertainment, information, and communicative expression. Prensky also offered the term "digital immigrants" to identify those who were *not* born into the generation that welcomed the Internet from the moment they arrived on Earth but nevertheless adapted to the influence of digital technology by either avoiding, accepting, or adopting it (see also Long 2005; McNeill 2009). By this definition, the first citizens of the Internet were digital immigrants (Baym 1993, 1995; Dorst 1990; Healy 1997; Hine 2000; Rheingold 2000; Turner 2008; see also Bennett, Maton, and Kervin 2008).

The terms "digital native" and "digital immigrant" may appear to be contentious—after all, there appears to be an implicit connotation of one group being superior to another. However, these terms are merely meant to represent a generational divide and not assess an ageist value judgment. Rhetoric aside, the reality is that younger generations are socialized into a world where continuous digital interconnectivity is prized. The widespread availability of new media and computer-mediated communication has fundamentally changed the ways in which people connect to the outside world and conceptualize their own personal worlds: instead of calling for directions to a local restaurant, people can now find the address online, enter it into their mobile device, and get step-by-step directions without bringing an external party into the process. Instead of waiting for their parents to finish the newspaper, children now must wait for their parents to check their e-mail. Instead of finding a stash of pornographic magazines nestled between their teenage son's mattress, parents must now eyeball computer files and Internet caches for clues on their child's naughty web-browsing habits. The culture continues to change.

While younger generations are immersed into this techno-savvy world from day one, the older generations that facilitated its growth in the first place have had to adapt to the increasingly fast and sophisticated pace set by the new generation of digital participants. I use the terms "digital native" and "immigrant" not to suggest an intellectual rift between those born before or after 1980 but rather to demarcate the "digital divide," after which technology became increasingly important (and eventually inseparable) in the social lives of Americans.

Throughout this work I employ the terms *analog* and *digital* to distinguish folkloric characteristics that are derived from the pre-Internet and current new media contexts, respectively.[2] "Digital" folklore is composed of virtualized, simulated, or otherwise physically intangible elements through computer-mediated communication technology. Further, it symbolically and cognitively replicates, complements, and enhances familiar components of corporeal interactions and conventions in the discourse of interaction. "Analog" is particularly sticky in that its historical context accurately implies a connection to the physical world, namely older broadcast mediums like television; for this reason, I also occasionally use "analog" to identify folklore that is rooted in "real world" or nondigital interactions. These are important terms to distinguish, as everything that is digitized has roots in the physical world, both in behavioral context as well as practice. After all, we all use analog equipment like computer monitors and keyboards to reach the digital expressive forum. It is essential to remember that there is always a human behind vernacular expression in new media contexts. In addition, we cannot understand the digital without first understanding its connection to the analog, both in its historical and pre-Internet sense as well as its modern usage as a description of "real world" interaction. Hence, the hybridization of folkloric behavior is a primary concern that I address throughout this work.

Readers may also note my occasional usage of *emic* and *etic*. These two terms are used in the humanities and social sciences to articulate how human behavior is reported by scholars. Emic refers to content that is consciously or subconsciously meaningful to the individual, and the informants' verbal or behavioral actions are interpreted and reported in ways that reflect an accurate "insider" perspective held by the culture or group that is being studied. The data that I refer to as having an emic context is meant to reflect the views and identity that are embodied while also underscoring its folk interactions and communally derived values. In these cases, I attempt to reveal how an individual within a particular context would explain their motivations. An etic account is the objective interpretation of a researcher, such as my prerogative to categorize or analyze cultural patterns that I observe in analog, digital, or hybridized contexts.

To illustrate the differences between emic and etic, take the example of a participant in an online forum who purposely posts nasty things and explains that their rationale for doing this was "to have fun." This informant's explanation would be considered emic, as it came directly from them and rhetorically represents their relationship to the communicative event. Additionally, subsequent forum responses by other participants who lambast the user's nasty rhetoric would also be emic. However, if I (as a researcher) were to analyze this interaction and conclude that it was simply an attempt to rhetorically seek out other like-minded individuals with disdain for a particular forum topic, this would be an etic account, since my interpretation is grounded in the analysis of a group's interaction and not derived from their own vocalized assertions.

Having objectively described the subject matter of this book, it is only appropriate that I declare my own, subjective intentions. Where do I, as an author, fit into this study? Why do I care? And given that my research is firmly entrenched in the study of new media and other emergent forms of folklore, why am I writing a *book*like manuscript instead of a newfangled, e-Something?

I am a digital native; I am a member of the generation that bore witness to the dawning of the digital age as it unfolded, evolved, and became a fixture of global society (Palvrey and Gasser 2008; Prensky 2001a; Tapscott 1999; Weber and Dixon 2007). Growing up, I experienced the unmistakable headaches induced by the droning hiss of a modem connecting, illegally downloaded music and movies into all hours of the night, and cruised for (and found) "Internet girlfriends" on AOL Instant Messenger. I received hundreds of e-mails that contained jokes, manipulated pictures, and requests for forwarding. I read the sanctimonious pontifications of amateur bloggers and laughed at the rhetoric of performance found on the individual user pages of Facebook, MySpace, and Wikipedia. I gazed in amazement as the clunky computer that once took up my father's office in 1984 became exponentially more powerful, compact, and connected to the surrounding world in the form of laptops, BlackBerries, or the latest model of the iPod, iPhone, and iPad. All of this took place in the last three decades, and every generation following mine will also be composed of digital natives who witness the continuing evolution of technology around them.

It is prudent to note that just as there are digital immigrants who reject or only begrudgingly adopt new media for communication and connectivity, not all digital natives are technological purists. Personally, I am a technological enthusiast, but in no way do I reject folklore from the "real" world (including contemporary folklore); it is likely that I will always favor the tangibility of holding a good book in my hands to reading one on a Nook or Kindle. I firmly believe that new media technologies (especially the Internet and mobile devices) invite and facilitate the transmission of the most current and ubiquitous folklore in circulation, but I am also cognizant of the fact that there is no time since digitization became possible that any given behavior or text online has not been a merger between analog and digital folklore forms. Indeed, the Internet supports and modifies the folk process by merging the familiarity of face-to-face cultural practices with the conveniences and conventions of online interaction. The process of creation comes more into public view and is open for commentary, whereas in the "real" world the product is less susceptible to communal commentary without direct solicitation. Issues of public and private domain are perpetually brought to the fore.

Even though I was born after Prensky's digital divide, the ways that people are using technology to express themselves nowadays—especially newer generations of participants—is under constant revision. I am interested in how the digital divide has influenced or complicated the ways in which folklore is transmitted and interpreted. This requires a long-term commitment to the continual study of new media, but the reality is that a time lag exists between a current event and the publication of a scholarly work. Even the "new" collected materials from this study will be quickly outdated as new forms and behaviors emerge online and through new media outlets. Furthermore, it is difficult to categorize or predict the exact methods by which an individual will communicate with others following a media disaster.

Methodologically, throughout this book I examine vernacular expression and the humorous discourse online as users encounter them: in various blogs, discussion forums, chat rooms, artistic sites, and message boards. I collect and report data collected on formal news sites (like newsweek.com or cnn.com) and commercial/entertainment/satire sites (such as tmz.com, theonion.com, and ebaumsworld.com), as well as individually moderated or locally conceived online venues and visual-oriented sites of expression such as YouTube.com, especially in the "comments" sections of these sites. In doing so, I look back specifically to potent moments in time surrounding tragedies and cultural scenes in an effort to explain the patterns of humor diffusion, the folk responses to the appropriateness of the humor's content, and how joke construction and content varied between the physical and digital worlds. I distinguish whether the websites are *static* (stable or unchanging in their display of content—such as in a list or grouped information that acts like an archive and does not allow for interactive discourse) or *dynamic* (ever-changing and malleable; soliciting participation, reception, and responses in real time). Although dynamic sites may ultimately become static after their relevancy has waned, the identification of contextual, Internet-based humor is crucial to accurately reporting and interpreting data on its dissemination and meaning (Laineste 2003).

While patterns regarding the content of humorous narratives are distinguishable over time, the means of communicating vernacular expression are in a state of constant flux. Technological ingenuity, coupled with the eager consumption and demand for increasingly complex devices that afford seamless connectivity to the Internet, complicates the definitive summation of the tools utilized by online participants. This is an impossible hurdle to overcome, but I nevertheless present my data in an effort to showcase the trajectory of folklore in the digital age with the hopes that such reportage will help future scholars to better contextualize their data and synthesize their approaches while simultaneously chronicling and interpreting the overarching components of popular culture.

In case it was not abundantly clear, my academic background is in folklore and American studies. I interpret cultural patterns and expressive behaviors through this lens, and more specifically from an Americanist perspective. This is my announced bias, and though I strive to be objective, my interpretations are informed by this intellectual purview. Unapologetically, this book emphasizes the relevancy of mass-mediated disasters from an Americanist perspective and my analysis is derived from and directed toward American culture. It is my hope that this work demonstrates one of the innumerable possibilities for future scholarship that is capable of juxtaposing the study of American culture and society in a productive dialogue regarding issues of mutual concern on the global stage. While I focus primarily on the responses to media events from within the borders of the United States and derive my observations from predominantly American informants, I believe that my methods and general observations on the contemporary patterns of vernacular expression online may be expanded upon in cross-cultural perspectives (see Ellis 2003). It bears noting that the United States ranks behind only China as the country with the most Internet users and boasts a 77.3 percent penetration rate among its citizens (Internet World Stats 2010).

Following the introduction, I begin with chapter 1, "Searching for Connections: How and Why We Use New Media for Vernacular Expression," in which I discuss the ways that new media now competes with other mediums to elicit folk responses and the historical contexts that facilitate contemporary traditions. In an effort to document the "real world" precedents regarding the folk responses to media disasters, and to provide the historical context about the folk responses to tragedy, I next examine media disasters in their face-to-face, corporeal contexts from local, regional, and national perspectives in chapter 2, "Changing Technologies, Changing Tastes: The Evolution of Humor and Mass-Mediated Disasters in the Late Twentieth Century." I begin by profiling the humor, narratives, and mediated responses from a variety of media disasters that occurred before the Internet was a popular mode of communication, namely the near-catastrophic accident at the Three Mile Island nuclear plant near Harrisburg, Pennsylvania, in 1979, and the Challenger space shuttle disaster. By revisiting these early examples of media-influenced folk humor, I aim to illustrate the historical precedence from which contemporary vernacular expression is derived.

Next, I map out the chronology of web-based humor forms and traditions and how they have evolved since their debut in the text- and frame-heavy interface of the Web 1.0 era in chapter 3, "From 9/11 to the Death of bin Laden: Vernacular Expression and the Emergence of Web 2.0." Following a brief overview of Web 1.0, I showcase the evolution of vernacular expression to mediated stimuli by first exploring the most-documented media disaster that garnered folk responses on the Internet: the terrorist attacks of September 11. From there, I explore how emergent technologies have played (and continue to play) an increasingly uncontestable role in how people process their behaviors and outlook stemming from emotional or contentious events. In addition to analyzing the folk response to the attacks and aftermath of 9/11, I also briefly profile the mass-mediated responses to the devastation of Hurricane Katrina in August 2005 and the BP oil spill of April 2010. Coming full circle, I close with an overview and examination of the Internet-derived humor and vernacular expression that vibrantly surfaced online after news broke that Osama bin Laden—the orchestrator behind the 9/11 attacks—was killed by U.S. Navy SEALS in Pakistan on April 29, 2011. Most important, I demonstrate how vernacular expression, particularly in aesthetic and visual forms, has notably evolved since 2001 and how these changes reflect upon the current trajectory of technologically mediated communication yet simultaneously reveal the Internet medium's traditionality.

It is important to note that mass-mediated disaster does not necessarily have to include a grandiose tragedy to trigger the psychological response patterns observed following large-scale disasters. In fact, any continuously reported, oversaturated news story that mirrors the same feelings of heightened anxiety and inescapability that often accompany the media coverage of a domestic tragedy can spark the same kinds of creative reactions that a massacre or natural disaster may elicit in contemporary folk culture, especially when the news event is perceived as shocking or disconcerting—even if the actual story is unrelated to a large-scale event.

To this end, chapter 4, "'Intimate Strangers': The Folk Response to Celebrity Death and Falls from Grace," documents contemporary examples of the folk response to media disasters on the World Wide Web through the lens of celebrity culture. The chapter serves as a thematic segue from the book's initial emphasis on the historical contexts and emergent trends of technologically mediated death and disaster humor and expression by applying my observations and analysis to the myriad ways in which people symbolically engage contemporary celebrity culture. While celebrities and the folk response to tragedy may not appear to be related on the surface, this chapter contemplates how individuals create imaginary pseudorelationships with celebrities in order to simulate greater connectivity with the surrounding world while soothing their own feelings of disconnectedness from their peers. I argue that the psychological function of such practices is analogous to the cognitive dissonance that people often experience during and after a traumatic event takes place (usually while attempting to soften the impact of the harrowing reality that surrounds them). The documentation of these patterns serves to fortify my argumentation regarding the psychological need to create humor in the face of psychological stress.

Celebrities are humanized through joking (see Barrick 1982), and so I use them as a thematic reference point that reveals the ways people vocalize their opinions through the Internet. In transitioning from a broader review of celebrity culture, I divert my analysis toward two specific folk response patterns and repertoires that surfaced in reaction to the erosion of support for once-revered celebrities such as golf pro Tiger Woods and music icon Michael Jackson. In many ways, the humorous narratives that surfaced in the wake of these celebrities' falls from grace helped to draw the dividing lines of taste and set the stage for a contentious, rhetorical battleground of vernacular expression in cyberspace. In chapter 5, "From Sports Hero to Supervillain: Or, How Tiger Woods Wrecked His Car(eer)," I interpret the meaning and function of humor created in response to news reportage on the graphic details about the extramarital exploits of golf pro Tiger Woods and the impact of his actions on his public persona. I conclude my analysis of celebrity humor and culture online with chapter 6, "Dethroning the King of Pop: Michael Jackson and the

Humor of Death," in which I analyze the folk response to the King of Pop's death in the days and months following its announcement and hypothesize as to how the posthumous parodies aimed at Jackson were influenced by the contextual events in popular culture that happened to occur around the same time that he passed away.

Having interpreted several specific humor cycles on the Internet, I bring everything together by discussing the notion of the Internet as a cyber*space* in chapter 7, "Laughing to Death: Tradition, Vernacular Expression, and American Culture in the Digital Age." More specifically, I discuss what kind of place it is, particularly to American users who engage in humor and other folkloric practices, and how the folk conceptualization of such meaningful, digitized convergence seemingly contributes to a simulative, "open" frontier for which different vernacular and corporate forces compete to dominate. In answering these questions, I summarize the larger points made throughout *The Last Laugh* regarding the importance of studying vernacular expression in cyberspace and its applicability in the study of contemporary folk cultures. Finally, I conclude the book with suggestions for new avenues for future studies and reiterate the importance of understanding humor as a part of the folk process and the larger expressive behaviors at work.

Engaging in participatory culture, either directly or through "lurking," is one of the most viable ways to make one's voice heard online today. Still, I am aware that I may be susceptible to criticism for focusing my research on a subversive topic such as death humor in cyberspace because of its controversial materials. While my research explores some taboo areas of folklore in contemporary society, I have taken great care to faithfully represent the various ways that people respond to media disasters in the digital world. As a result, the data is not always classy or politically correct, but it is nevertheless accurate and representative of emergent trends in vernacular expression. Some of the humor and narratives that I analyze are irreverent or just plain mean; others are sad, shocking, or bittersweet. But at the end of the day, whether you are a digital native or digital immigrant, my interpretation and analysis of contemporary vernacular expression demonstrates the new ways that people interact with Internet technologies.

Acknowledgments

Writer and humorist Robert Benchley once quipped that "defining and analyzing humor is a pastime of humorless people." While the study of disaster may not be the most cheery subject on the surface, this project has been a real labor of love. Between the many hours of solitude that I spent in the dark corners of libraries or sifting through endless scholarly articles at the office, there were many people who donated their time, energy, and kindness to me in the process of completing this book. I am honored to count them as friends.

First and foremost, my wife and soul mate, Angelina, has been a constant source of love, happiness, and humor since we met, and I am so grateful to have her as my partner and pillar of support. Her unwavering enthusiasm for my work—even after the many hours, days, and nights that I spent plugging away at it in an empty, lonely corner of our home—has been a welcome and wonderful reprieve from the grind. My parents, Bruce and Anita; my sister, Natalie; and my fantastic in-laws, Phil, Laura, and Christy Sanfilippo and Rick and Janie Miller, have all been great (as usual) and have supported me and provided many days of pleasant distraction. Also, of course, my delightful Beagle mix, Penny, has always offered her affection whenever I felt frazzled.

I wish to thank and recognize my mentor, Simon J. Bronner—to whom this work is dedicated—whose guidance, patience, and generosity have been invaluable during the completion of this research. Simon has been instrumental in shaping the trajectory of my research interests, and I am thankful for his interest and commitment to deepening my understanding and appreciation for the study of American folklore and folklife. Above all, he has played a crucial role in my intellectual development and has shown great faith in my numerous projects, even those that fell within the outskirts of typical scholarly inquiry. I am grateful for his support, and I know that any student would be lucky to call him a friend and mentor. I am also indebted to Michael Barton, John Haddad, Charles Kupfer, and Girish Subramanian for their service, dedication, and helpful suggestions throughout the completion of this manuscript.

There is no doubt in my mind that this work could not have been successfully completed without the astute eye and rational opinions of several outstanding scholars who graciously donated their time in reviewing several early versions of chapters within this work. As such, I would like to extend a special thank-you to my friends and colleagues Erika Brady, Rebekah Burchfield, Celia Cain, Jennifer Dutch, Elaine Eff, Tim Evans, Craig Gill, Sandra Grady, Spencer Lincoln Green, Julia Kelso, Laurie Matheson, Judith McCulloh, Mark Miyake, and Leonard Primiano. I owe a special thanks to Elizabeth Tucker, who really went above and beyond in extending her time and generosity in both this endeavor as well as other scholarly pursuits. I am also grateful to Donald Allport Bird, Charley Camp, Patrick Clarke, Bill Ellis, Gary Alan Fine, Stephen Olbrys Gencarella, Lindsay Harlow, Robert Glenn Howard, Michael Owen Jones, Lynne S. McNeill, Montana Miller, David Puglia, Steve Stanzak, Tok Thompson, and Jeff Tolbert for their time and useful comments on early ideas and trajectories that have permeated this book.

At the ripe old age of ten, I can recall promising myself that I would someday only pursue a career in a line of work that could make me truly happy. Nearly two decades later, I am so thankful and honored to have found such a calling in the study of folklore. Many of my students smile from ear to ear whenever I tell them about the work of folklorists, and it is a true privilege to be a member of this discipline. For this project, and for the many that preceded it (and those that will follow), I owe a debt of gratitude to the American Folklore Society and its constituents. The organization's enthusiastic support of my research at conferences and workshops has been invaluable for the completion of this manuscript. The challenging and thought-provoking conversations that took place during annual meetings and other allied events have been incredibly beneficial.

In some ways, many of the chapters for this book were approached as "mini research projects," and numerous colleagues are due thanks for their support and advice in the development of this work. Some case studies struck closer to the heart than others. I completed my PhD at Penn State Harrisburg, which is located in Middletown, Pennsylvania—just a few miles from Three Mile Island—and as such, a considerable amount of personal stake (both for my program and myself as well as the people of the surrounding community) was invested in the respectful presentation of Three Mile Island folklore, retrospectively. In researching and collecting information on the accident and the aftermath, I am indebted to the incredible staff at the Pennsylvania State University Harrisburg library and the Archives of Folklore and Ethnography at Penn State Harrisburg, especially Heidi Abbey, Alan E. Mays, and Fay Youngmark, for their time, effort, and enthusiasm in helping me uncover and/or duplicate delicate artifacts stemming from the Three Mile Island accident. Folklorist Yvonne Milspaw was generous with her time and knowledge of Three Mile Island folklore and humor.

There are many good folks who have been a joy to know and work with before, during, and after the completion of this project whom I would like to recognize: Jennie Adams, Jade Alburo, John Alley, Cathy and Ronald Baker, Warren Belasco, Gabi Berlinger, Kristen Bradley, Chet Breaux, Ian Brodie, Anthony Bak Buccitelli, Rebekah Burchfield, Sally Hogan Clark, Bridgette Dembowski, Susan Eckelmann, M. Rachel Gholson, Joseph Goodwin, Nicholas Gotwalt, Jonathan Gray, Fredara Hadley, Aaron Harms, Brenna Heffner, John Heflin, Darcy Holtgrave, Suzanne Godsby Ingalsbe, Jason Jackson, Pat Johnson, Jeana Jorgensen, Merrill Kaplan, Andrea Kitta, Jen Laherty, Kara Lairson, Zach Langley, Mark Layser, Justin Levy, Tim Lloyd, Joanne Magee, John H. McDowell, Jim McMahon, Carol McQuiggan, Jay Mechling, Amy Milligan, Selina Morales, Elliott Oring, Ed Orser, Susan Ortmann, Jodine Perkins, Sheila Rohrer, Jared Rife, Katie Robinson, Kate Schramm, Jim Seaver, Moira Smith, Jenni Spitulnik-Hughes, Kristiana Willsey, and Adam Zolkover. Without them, this work would have been a much more lonesome task to complete. I would also like to thank all of my colleagues in the Department of English and Communication at SUNY Potsdam for welcoming me to the North Country, especially Pam Cullen, Jim Donahue, Christine Doran, Marilyn Fayette, David Fregoe, Rick Henry, Christina Knopf, Joanna Luloff, Steve Marqusee, Derek Maus, Donald McNutt, Jennifer Mitchell, Bethany Newhall, Sue Novak, Liberty Stanavage, and John Youngblood.

Last, but certainly not least, I wish to express my gratitude to Sheila Leary and the wonderful staff at the University of Wisconsin Press for their time and dedication to the continued development and successful completion of this manuscript. I am humbled to have been selected by the press to participate in the Folklore in a Multicultural World series and honored to present my research under such auspices. It has been a tremendous privilege to work with them, and I am certain that the end result has greatly benefited from their guiding hand.

The Last Laugh

Introduction

CYBERSPACE, TECHNOLOGY, AND MASS MEDIA
IN THE TWENTY-FIRST CENTURY

June 25, 2009, began as a normal day. I was in Bloomington, Indiana, teaching an introductory folklore class (cleverly disguised as a sociology course) for the local community college. About an hour into our discussion, one of my students' phones began to vibrate loudly. I leveled him with a stern "teacher's glare" as he silenced his phone, but not even a minute later his phone vibrated again—and this time he checked it right in front of me. Before I had the chance to dropkick him for disrupting class, he raised his hand and sheepishly stammered, "I don't mean to interrupt . . . but I just got a text that Michael Jackson died." Audible gasps could be heard throughout the class, followed almost immediately by personal commentaries on the nature of the situation being disheartening, untimely, unfortunate, or—in some cases—quite humorous. Within seconds of the news first breaking, my classroom devolved into a late-night comedy forum: "They're gonna need a jackhammer to do the autopsy on his plastic ass," exclaimed one student. "I wonder if anyone will moonwalk past the casket for good luck," offered another.

Before even two minutes had passed from the initial interruption, something fascinating took place in my classroom: as if witnessing a virus spread, another student's phone vibrated. Then another. And then another. Within five minutes, all but one of my fifteen students' phones had vibrated and all of them reported receiving text messages that relayed that Michael Jackson had died. At that moment I realized that I was witnessing a unique moment of folkloric dissemination made possible by the digital age.

I suspended our class lesson and took to the Internet with my students to see if we could be the first to report of Michael Jackson's passing on the folk-moderated digital encyclopedia, Wikipedia. However, by the time the page loaded we were surprised to find that a full, detailed article had already been posted with a userbox caveat noting that the article "refers to a person who has recently died. Some information, such as that pertaining to the circumstances of the person's death and surrounding events, may change as more facts become known."[1] A quick trip to Google thereafter with the search criteria "Michael Jackson" nearly froze the computer—it was later confirmed by researchers that the news of Jackson's passing had spread so quickly that the immense swell of participants seeking information on the Web had caused the infrastructure to slow to a crawl, nearly "breaking" the Internet and disrupting numerous websites and electronic media sites and services such as Twitter and Google News (Rawlinson and Hunt 2009).[2] As it turned out, June 25, 2009, was a memorable day after all.

My experience and my students' experiences in the moments following the death of Michael Jackson exemplify contemporary American culture's high-tech, fast-paced behavioral response to salacious or tragic stories that hit the newsfeed. Today people are perpetually connected to the digital format. Information constantly flows to users, and there is never a break in coverage. From twenty-four-hour news stations and Internet news sites to information collected from friends' Twitter updates and personal text messages, a major news story never stays unnoticed or uncommented upon for long.

Sociologist David Riesman posits in his classic work, *The Lonely Crowd* (1950), that American character has shifted from being tradition directed (guided by the predominant values and practices of previous generations) to inner directed (guided by an "internal gyroscope" that leads the individual to define their own set of values). Following the Industrial Revolution, an economically stable "middle class" emerged in America that caused individuals to migrate toward an "other-directed" mentality guided by the need to meaningfully relate to (or distinguish oneself from) peers. While earlier generations were said to have been motivated by the need to produce and conserve scarce materials, the other-directed society was motivated by the need to consume as act of social participation. Material acquisitions and outward expressions of creativity symbolized the individuals' connection with mass society.

Even though some traditions may no longer guide specific modes of social interaction, they nevertheless inform the ways that vernacular expression manifests itself in modern society. As older patterns of socialization fade, they inevitably reemerge in modified ways. Computer-mediated communication technologies provide users guided by tradition-, inner-, or other-directed personalities with a forum that can adapt to their individual needs for symbolic expression while providing a simulated sense of connectivity to the outside world. People inherently need to feel connected or united with others in some way—especially in times of social anxiety or forced emotional suppression—and the Internet and other new media technologies deeply fulfill these needs. At its best, this technology provides an expansive forum for humorous, combative, or intellectual communicative exchanges and other rhetoric that help participants to feel as though they are a part of something meaningful.

In oral traditions of "tasteless," "sick," or "gross" humor before the digital age, the majority of jokesters were male adolescents (Bronner 1985; see also Blank 2010; Bronner 1995; Ellis 1991, 117; Fine and Johnson 1980; Leary 1977; Oring 1992; Samuelson 1995; Smyth 1986). In "pre-Internet" work environments, especially those where employees frequently interacted with computer technologies, hand-drawn or photocopied replications of folklore were often circulated anonymously and consumed by a wider—albeit homogeneous—audience (Barrick 1972; Dundes and Pagter [1975] 1978; Preston 1994). But as the Internet developed into an affordable, usable, and obtainable commodity (accessible via numerous portable communication devices), a more diverse and widespread body of users adopted these technologies into their everyday lives. Consequently, the online venue came to serve as a key breeding ground for folkloric dissemination by providing greater accessibility for users to engage and circulate traditional expressive forms in newfangled ways.[3]

Communications scholar Marshall McLuhan (1964, 1967) famously suggested that there are perceptive differences between forms of "hot" media (that which demand viewers' visual attention but do not require active participation, as with watching a movie) and "cool" media (that which requires audiences' deeper, conscious participation, such as reading a book). In the words of folklorist Paul Smith, "the personal computer is the equivalent of a typewriter, photocopier and communications device—all rolled into one" (1991, 267)—and now, so much more. The Internet combines "hot" and "cool" cognitive stimulation by juxtaposing the medium's visuality with the highly interactive textual and artistic outlets, like with YouTube (which combines audiovisual stimuli with the ability to comment on posted material or other user comments). But how and why does the Internet facilitate such vast digital symbolic interaction today? Moreover, how do folkloric texts differ from (or preserve) the ways in which individuals and their communities would respond to death, disaster, and scandal *before* the digital age? And what does all of this suggest about the function of folklore in times of peril?

The context of the medium through which symbolic communication takes place is undoubtedly important, but the behavioral component of communication—the subtexts of interactive rhetoric, the motivations behind a person's willingness to engage an online community at four in the morning while their whole family sleeps, and the ways that symbolic interaction results in semiotic translations from one domain to another—reveals the most salient information about people and expressive tendencies today.

The Cultural Inventory as Storehouse for Folk Knowledge

In most of our social relationships, we can choose whom we associate with. We decide our preferences for the kinds of entertainment that we find pleasurable, just as we decide on the educational or career trajectory that seems suitable for our goals in life. All of these choices reflect our own intrinsic values, but they also speak to our greater need for social interaction. We do this because it is human nature to desire connectivity with other people, to build relationships, and to contribute to a valuable existence within society. In fact, the absence of such desires is often treated as a sign of psychological disruption. We are socially conditioned to accept or pursue these tasks as social beings. Our memories of these pursuits and our interactions that form as resulting constructs make up the master narratives of our lives. In short, we strive to cultivate a meaningful existence through symbolic positioning of our memories and management of social relationships, socioeconomic statuses, and our roles within our communities as markers of self-worth and measurement of accomplishment toward the goal of productivity. These markers for success are contextual and vary depending on individual experiences and/or community expectations, which are often steeped in a lineage of tradition that provides quiet stability.

In our everyday interactions, even those with strangers, we bring all of our social and contextual baggage with us for better or worse. Our word choices and pronunciations, our jokes, our ideas of good taste, our beliefs in appropriate displays of public affection, our political ideologies, our favorite songs, our expectations of how to treat one another or how to handle a disagreement—all of these preferences, expectations, and actions that they produce are a result of our experiences and the contextual, social influences that have been bestowed upon us. Our view of the world and how we fit into it is informed by our notion of the meaningful traditions to which we belong. In the words of sociologist Erving Goffman, "Life may not be an imitation of art, but ordinary conduct, in a sense, is an imitation of the proprieties, a gesture at the exemplary forms, and the primal realization of these ideals belongs more to make-believe than to reality" (1974, 562). Indeed, the values and expectations that we assign to a given entity or idea reflect the worldviews we have individually accumulated and nurtured throughout a lifetime's worth of symbolic interaction with peers, folk and popular culture, and the mass media (Vygotsky 1978; see also Berger and Luckmann 1966; Dundes 1971). This subconscious acquisition of cultural symbols and meanings, value determinations, and folk knowledge inform our *cultural inventory*, or the contextual frames of reference we use to reconcile our individual ideas, values, beliefs, and experiences (both personal and fabricated through symbolic interaction in face-to-face and online settings) when faced with incongruities in everyday life. When deployed in social and interactive settings, it can be used to reveal common ground and promote group cohesion.

The cultural inventory is a cognitive storehouse of knowledge that compartmentalizes memories and values assigned to the meaningful symbols in culture and society for easy access. In essence, it serves as a psychological filter for interpreting communicative events; oftentimes it is shaped by the intersection of folk and popular culture and, consequently, contains referential ties to film, television, or religion as a means of making sense of social situations and public personas. Much like browsing through a catalog, we attach values to images, motifs, and themes found in quasi-similar materials from folk and popular culture. When reading a news story of a child's frightful race down a steep mountain in an effort to escape the path of a large, tumbling boulder, we might instantly remember a scene from *Raiders of the Lost Ark* (1981) to provide some sense of connection or understanding to the story itself (or perhaps some nervous comic relief). As a result, we also manage to dilute the seriousness of the actual event's near-tragic conclusion via a neatly packaged play frame that relies on the fantastical, fictional symbol of reference to neutralize our instinctive emotional response. We create narratives of these events to better understand and contextualize their gravity and develop our appropriate roles in the story.[4]

But what happens if we are not able to brush off the seriousness of a tragedy by simply utilizing our cultural inventory? Can our knowledge of popular culture motifs or other symbolic imagery from the mass media actually impede our pursuit of tempering the stress of an unfolding disaster?

Humor, Disaster, and the Cognitive Organization of Mass-Mediated Folklore

Jim Morrison, legendary front man of the 1960s rock group The Doors, once said that "whoever controls the media, controls the mind." Cynicism aside, there is some truth to the statement in that (generally speaking) the mass media's coverage of disaster is greatly disproportionate to the amount of "straight news" stories that are reported (Singer and Endremy 1993; see also Barton 1998). When reportage of a crisis or tragedy becomes inescapable, a chain reaction of narrative dissemination invades the cognitive awareness of the majority of American citizens. The phenomenon of a "media disaster" (or mass-mediated disaster) takes place and invites media viewers to consume and reproduce sentiments about the event to others quickly (Ellis 2001). Informed citizens are expected to symbolically express their solidarity with those affected by the pending crisis through showing emotion, engaging in rhetorical exchange, or by donating time and money toward a resolution or comparable alleviatory effort. Such intense media coverage has spawned notable psychological repercussions such as "media disaster syndrome" (Wolfenstein and Kliman 1965) whereby viewers cannot escape the news story and thus are forced to cope through finding solace in symbolic interaction or connectivity with others.

Perhaps one of the most important yet underappreciated aspects of the Internet venue during tumultuous times is its liminality—an ambivalent state of existence that is neither physical nor truly intangible (V. Turner 1974; see also Danet 2001, 8; Jones, Zagacki, and Lewis 2007).[5] Users on the Internet are "betwixt and between" modes of corporeality and intangibility by the very nature of the venue's simulative interface. Thus, according to philosopher Jean Baudrillard (1995), what constitutes "reality" is only that which the individual cognitively perceives to be real—a task that is becoming increasingly difficult because of the overreliance on the media for assigning symbols to replace concrete ideas and practices.[6] The expressive forums found throughout the Internet foster a sense of belonging and connection to the outside world. Many online communities facilitate what Henry Jenkins has referred to as a *participatory culture*, or "a culture with relatively low barriers to artistic expression and civic engagement, strong support for creating and sharing creations, and some type of informal mentorship whereby experienced participants pass along knowledge to novices," adding that these are places where "members also believe their contributions matter and feel some degree of social connection with one another (at the least, members care about others' opinions of what they have created)" (Jenkins et al. 2009, xi; see also Howard 2008b; Jenkins 2006, 2008).

Mass-mediated disasters can occur following a nationally televised tragedy (as with the Challenger space shuttle disaster), a terrorist attack (as was the case after 9/11), a natural disaster (after Hurricane Katrina), or even following the death of an internationally renowned celebrity, such as entertainers Elvis Presley or, more recently, Michael Jackson (see Couldry, Hepp, and Kotz 2009). Significant social changes that are ongoing, as was the case with the

Civil Rights and Women's Liberation movements during the Vietnam era, have also been quite capable of stirring a vibrant public discourse about issues that concern Americans.[7] As media consumers reach critical mass they seek common ground with the surrounding world, often in rejection of the emotional hegemony of commercial media outlets.

What society takes most seriously—death—also leads ironically to the predominant theme of humor, and in the construction of humor about death, the role of the living is most frequently at issue. The paradox of life (namely that it must end) often informs the folk response to disaster and tragedy (see Narváez 2003). As folklorist Willie Smyth articulates, jokes "may function to discharge the psychic energy connected with [death] by providing a channel through which the anxiety attached to a thought of a catastrophic event may be diverted" (1986, 254). Thus, in the wake of an emotionally traumatic event the combination of the two opposing themes helps to release anxieties about mortality by making a serious topic into a pleasurable one. Joking gives people the ability to withstand the stress of tragic events while enabling mass culture to resist the constraints of the emotional control imposed by the media following a tragedy. Humorous expression and other symbolic rhetoric often surfaces in order to alleviate the tensions that may arise from the social anxieties at hand. But why else does this happen?

Sociologist Christie Davies suggests that the "driving force behind the popularity of disaster jokes is the emotional hegemony [or total dominance over a medium[8]] enjoyed by those controlling television, who feel able to tell viewers what to feel" (2003, 26). Viewers deliberately take to the Internet in direct opposition to the sentiments conveyed through traditional telecommunicated media outlets in an effort to express their anxieties and to alleviate the stresses conjured up by media oversaturation through the use of humor and narrative transmission. To this end, the increased institutionalization of the grieving process becomes inexorably linked with the folk resentment over the ways in which we learn about "bad news" (Ellis 2001, 3; see also Oring 1987; Simons 1986).

More than most psychological defense mechanisms, jokes require a delicate balance between the sensibilities of the audience and the joke-teller (Fine 1988, 177). Folklorist Moira Smith notes that "those who tell a joke must balance the potential benefits they stand to reap by provoking mirth with the social risk of telling an unfunny or sick joke" (1990, 96). Joke telling involves the calculated risk of performing humor litigiously in an effort to yield positive feedback. The level of success often corresponds to the proximity of the audience to the subject of ridicule. But as with the earlier technologically mediated communication devices from the paperwork empire, the purveyors of folkloric expression on the Internet are also often anonymously authored. Similarly, online discourse encourages the circulation of bawdy humor unhindered by the coded expectations of social decorum.

In addition to regular joke-tellers, hate-mongering entities have at times organized online under the guise of cleverly devised websites that espouse racist and xenophobic humorous and inflammatory rhetoric (see Blank 2009c). But more generally, ethnic jokes that were once taciturnly shared in the corporeal world now appear on numerous formal joke sites, not to mention the comments section of "regular" websites that do not even seek out such dialogue. The transposition of jokes from older joke contexts (both in terms of origin as well as the antecedent intention for its comedic effect) demonstrates the traditionality of hybridized folklore in the digital age. For example, the joke "What do they call a [black person] with a PhD in Mississippi?" (the answer: "Nigger") first surfaced during the Civil Rights era in response to whites' anxiety about ongoing social change (see Abrahams and Dundes 1969, 238; Dundes 1987a; Kennedy 2003, 29; Lewis 2006, 117; Oring 1992, 18). However, through repetition and variation, this joke resurfaced online shortly after Harvard professor Henry Louis Gates, an African American, was arrested under the suspicion of burglary and disorderly conduct while unsuccessfully attempting to enter his own home in July 2009 (Thompson 2009).[9]

Gates's reputation as a respected scholar garnered media scrutiny to the arrest, but his accusations of racial profiling against the arresting officers of the Cambridge, Massachusetts, Police Department really got things rolling. The story of Gates's arrest, coupled with the ongoing media attention paid to the relatively recent inauguration of America's first black president, Barack Obama, encouraged media pundits to ruminate about racial tensions in America and the current status of African Americans within society. Thus, the motivation informing the original joke—to alleviate white anxiety over black empowerment through derogatory humor—was updated to accommodate new and resurfacing anxieties about race and the sympathetic treatment of minorities in the media.

The reintegration of oral traditions and other forms of "analog" folklore into the digital medium is a ubiquitous occurrence; a hybridization of expressive behaviors across face-to-face and virtual contexts has developed as a result. But humor, which so often relies on performative cues and contexts, may appear trickier to identify or authenticate as genuine folklore online, given the medium's highly visual and text-oriented communication interfaces and ease with which one may cut, paste, and disseminate materials. To this end, Elliott

Oring comments that "a Web site for humor is not like the oral repertoire of an individual or group. Oral tradition operates editorially. Those jokes that do not meet the standards of an individual or group tend to be transformed or eliminated from the repertoire. The site may be managed for quantity rather than quality. It is an accumulation that may not reflect the aesthetics or ideology of any individual or group. Consequently, anything that might qualify as . . . humor might be posted at the site (2003, 139; see also Davies 2003, 2011). Oring presumes an analog definition of folkloric creation in oral transmission, but the aggregation of material—what Simon Bronner (2009) describes as the analytic or digital definition of folklore in repetition and variation—provides an important cultural practice in everyday life. Furthermore, as Barbara Kirshemblatt-Gimblett notes, "The very technologies that threaten to displace oral traditions are also the instruments for preserving them" (1995, 70; reiterated and also quoted in Blank 2009a, 12).

The traditions of older materials find new value in the present and are thereupon adopted as a hybridized entity. But more germane to this book is the fact that all the folkloric expressions that materialize after a tragedy provide some sort of pleasure or relief for those who engage in their dissemination or collection. After all, when the threat of death, harm, or loss looms, people instinctively seek out psychological outlets to affirm that they are not alone in their distress and to find ways to cope with the mounting pressures that surround them. New media technology helps to calm such pressures. By closely following a significant disaster or world event, media consumers establish a sense of stability from their newfound awareness, which they then use to anticipate or rationalize the causational anxieties that may surface in times of peril. However, when television news operations fall short of providing such comfort through their broadcasts (or conversely, when they devote too much time to a single news story and flood their programs with recycled facts that fail to advance the current state of knowledge), people individually seek out information through the use of technology in an attempt to make sense of the world as it changes—on their own terms.

Prior to the Internet's existence, most technologically mediated communicative receptions in mass society were passively disseminated; that is, they did not usually host contemporaneous expressive interactions like instant messaging or texting but rather a sender and a receiver, who need not directly communicate to convey a message. Despite this, the pervasiveness of television news and "live" reporting promoted a sense of simultaneity for viewers who were symbolically connecting to the events unfolding on the screen. Thus, the burgeoning Internet's most profound feature was its tremendous interactive content and the implicit idea that every person could be his or her own broadcaster. Rather expectedly, then, the interactivity of the online medium can become a powerful, personalized instrument of expression; almost anyone can assume the role of an amateur journalist or pundit. Participants' rhetorical investment in shaping the narrative of an ongoing news event inculcates a semblance of communal unity and connectivity amid an uncertain aftermath. The perpetual and ubiquitous availability of the Internet is a cultural "night light"—comforting those who seek the calming glow of its companionship in times of darkness and confusion.

The Internet propels the diffusion of humor about tragedies to many people who would not have been included in previous years. Disaster becomes immediate and accelerates rather than defuses the psychological need to create humor. In the absence of the social cues or communal approval that is customary to the physical realm, one must go to greater lengths to symbolically show their solidarity with their digital comrades, especially after a news event penetrates the fabric of an online community's perceived reach.

Disasters also provide a great case study of "folk process" because of the commentary and often ritualized elaboration (whether in mourning or humor) that they elicit. When mass-mediated disasters appear, people use the Internet and other new media devices not only to acquire new information on the situation at-hand but also to release their psychological angst and forge a symbolic unity through simulated interactivity online. Folklore is a vehicle for expression, and it lends itself to the ensuing discourse following an accident or disaster because community-generated humor, rumors, narratives, and other symbolic creations are used in the response to a perceived crisis. These symbolic, often humorous interactions—which are influenced by information and observed behaviors derived from the individual's absorption of folk and popular culture—reflexively project the nuances of human behavior in the response to social anxiety (see Correll 1997).

The response to disaster also provides credence to the theory that folklore serves as a means of escape, validation, education, and social control, with the goal of stabilizing society (Bascom 1954; see also Oring 1976). The transmission of folklore—traditional knowledge, beliefs, and customs—is no longer limited to vertical knowledge hierarchies that require a "handing down" or "handing up" of information through oral tradition or literature for information to pass. The remote and disembodied nature of cyberspace encourages and expects a democratic, *horizontal* diffusion of folk culture in which all participants are capable of forging a unique niche within their respective communities. Thus, folklore on the Internet reveals keen insights into the cultural ramifications of the digital age.

Nowadays, Americans are raised to seek and sustain intimacy with others through the use of computer-mediated communication. Social networking, texting, and online games are now among the most prevalent means of developing interpersonal communication skills and maintaining relationships with peers. Friends and family stay in touch with each other throughout the day by sending 144-character messages or sharing pictures and stories about their recent activities on Facebook and Twitter. As a result, many individuals' physical detachment from their "real world" communities is being compensated for through greater psychological attachment to others through the digital format, but questions remain. What are the cultural and psychological implications of such immense connectivity when extrapolated to the never-ending onslaught of information dissemination and retrieval that occurs in contemporary American culture? And what does it mean when these channels are tapped in the response to a crisis or unsavory news?

Without question, technology has fundamentally altered the ways in which people express themselves, as well as the ways that people negotiate the presentation of their identities in contemporary society. More so than other events, shocking news of death, disaster, and scandal invite humorous vernacular expression on the Internet when repetitively consumed via mass media outlets. It is essential that folklorists continue to examine the new ways in which people respond to significant, momentous events in contemporary society and contemplate how cyberspace has become the go-to format for vernacular expression. The study of how people respond to tragedy with humor *now*, in the digital age—with all of its methodological constraints and benefits, the complex questions that it inspires about how we express ourselves in contemporary society, and the convergent behaviors that hybridize the very displays of community and identity that folklorists have examined for decades—has immediate value and currency in the study of human communication.

The late Alan Dundes made scholarly waves in 1977 by declaring that "technology isn't stamping out folklore; rather it is becoming a vital factor in the transmission of folklore" (1980, 17), and he challenged folklorists to explore content that existed outside of orality. Following Dundes's inspiring call to explore technologically mediated folklore, *The Last Laugh* documents the technologically mediated expressive modes of the past and present in an effort to provide new insights into the ways that folklore thrives in a world of computer-mediated communication—especially following a death, disaster, or shocking event. In doing so, the book aims to challenge the conventional wisdom in folkloristics regarding the scholastic validity of cyberethnography and the data it yields. Humbly, it is my sincerest hope that my efforts here may serve to further open the door for future scholarship on this growing and important area of folkloristic inquiry.

CHAPTER I

◆

Searching for Connections

HOW AND WHY WE USE NEW MEDIA
FOR VERNACULAR EXPRESSION

For the first few years of my life I struggled to contort my lips into the shapes that would allow me to pronounce the official name for one of the first "toys" that I came to know and understand as a human being. Despite my developmental limitations, I would point to the bulky machine in my father's office while repeatedly uttering one of the first words that came from my mouth, "ahkaboo." While I have no actual memory of doing such things, I have seen the home videos from my childhood where I—a shaggy-haired little boy in a Michael Jackson T-shirt and red corduroy pants—point at the whirling lights, looking back at the camera with a cheesy grin, enamored by the glowing green phosphorous on the screen towering above my head and fascinated with the screeching sounds coming from an old dot-matrix printer. My parents came to realize that my pointing and repetition of "ahkaboo" was an infantile attempt at saying "computer."

As a digital native, to use Prensky's (2001a) term, I do not need to actually remember these events to know that computers have always been an integral part of my education, socialization, and development. Over time, my simple "ahkaboo" machine grew in importance—for information dissemination, mail, news, and work. It became an appliance every bit as important in my world as the refrigerator or television. Computer technology has profoundly influenced the ways that the world conducts its personal and commercial business. Digital natives and immigrants alike have become accustomed to the instantaneity and limitless barriers surrounding entertainment that is currently available at their fingertips.

Indubitably, the road to creating the modern day Internet technology we know today began long before I was born. However, before we can fully understand the influence of mass media on vernacular expression in the digital age, it is necessary to first broach upon the historical contexts from which contemporary computer-mediated communications have emerged as they influence and inform the folk response to death, disaster, and scandal. Doing so helps to ascertain technology's influence on the ways that people now attempt to acquire knowledge and emotional connectivity with others—especially in times of social anxiety.

Technology and the Transmission of Knowledge

The twenty-first-century cultural phenomenon of unimpeded connectivity and the constant barrage of information dissemination is arguably unique. Nevertheless, the expressive forms that emerge in response to information retrieval have distinguishable roots in the past. Before the Internet and new media changed the ways that society conceptualized boundaries of community, human connectivity, and knowledge, television and radio complicated the ways that people retrieved news and information by asserting hegemonic control over the emotionality of the news. Before that, newspapers and other print media reigned supreme in juxtaposition with the dissemination and acquisition of knowledge through oral tradition. But even these technologies owe their power to technological innovation throughout history.

In the grandest sense of the word, Johannes Gutenberg's introduction of the modern printing press in 1439 revolutionized the way that information and knowledge was subsequently shared and passed through textual replication. By the late fifteenth century, early news sheets (or broadsides) were surfacing in Germany, and more books were entering the marketplace throughout the major cities of Europe. In colonial America, British rulers were suppressing early efforts to create a widely read news publication. However, by the eve of the Revolutionary War several newspapers (see fig. 1) were able to garner support for independence (see Emery 1978). Indeed, freedom of the press was a major component of the United States' Bill of Rights (ratified in 1791), and the medium's use as a purveyor of news, opinion, and symbolism made it a vital institution in the development of early American ideology.

In the years to follow, American technological progress boomed in step with westward expansion during the Jacksonian Age. In addition to the tremendous increase in modes of transportation—namely the transcontinental railroad—as well as better roads and water passages, the invention of the steam-powered rotary press and the introduction of the electric telegraph significantly improved and empowered communication technology. Domestic and global communication became a reality. Interchangeable, standardized parts, or the "American

Figure 1. This political cartoon, Benjamin Franklin's infamous "Join, or Die" calling for colonial unity against British rule, originally appeared in the *Pennsylvania Gazette*, May 7, 1754. It was reprinted many times—and in many different publications—in the years to follow.

system of manufactures," influenced the development of machine technology such as the sewing machine and other mechanized tools by intentionally designing them to be capable of using parts that could be swapped in or out, which made any repairs or modifications to a machine significantly cheaper. This also hastened the advancement of communication technologies that were dependent on intricate, cooperative mechanics to operate efficiently (Hounsell 1984).[1] Most important, the growing association of information technology with the promotion of popular freedom held mass appeal (see Barth 1982; Boorstin 1974).

With technological progress came greater accessibility to information for many Americans, especially those who lived in urban centers. Newspapers had to distinguish themselves as reliable and entertaining to remain of interest to potential readers. Certainly, the attraction to salacious news stories and glamorized narratives found in today's mass-mediated society is a cultural reverberation of the sensationalist reporting tactics used by competing newspaper and magazine publishers, dime novelists, and "trash literature" that popularly circulated beginning in the 1830s and 1840s (see Goetzmann 2009). Perhaps most famously, William Randolph Hearst and Joseph Pulitzer's printing of "yellow journalism" raised the stakes of news stories by blurring the boundaries of fact and sensationalism through dramatic prose that incited hostility toward Spain (prior to the Spanish-American War) with stories of their colonial atrocities (Peceny 1997). Indeed, Hearst and Pulitzer's approaches—rooted in storytelling and the pleasure derived from the intelligent unpacking of a representative narrative—had a lasting impact on reporting and the organization of media events in the press during this era (Campbell 2003, 2006; Whyte 2009).

Before World War I, American news stories were written and presented in a way that could be described as "emotional," and often included gory details with strong attention to the narrative element of a news story instead of just delivering the facts (see Barton 1998). The newspapers of the late nineteenth century (and later the radio broadcasts of the early to mid-twentieth century) resembled our modern-day op-ed column in that they sought to engage larger issues through a representative, symbolic conduit. They were meant to represent the voice of the folk by using rhetoric as an emotional connecting point that linked readers to a shared ideological community. It was not until after the war that newspapers became more corporatized and predominantly moved toward the reportage of "straight news" stories that practiced restraint in sharing the unsavory nuances of a story. Emotionality and sensationalism were left to the burgeoning radio and television mediums.

By the mid-twentieth century, television broadcasting supplanted the newspaper as the predominant means of information retrieval and entertainment in American culture. By 1957 televisions were in 85 percent of American homes; that number would climb to 98 percent by the early 1980s (Cullen 2002, 205). With the television medium came a new opportunity for emotional solicitation and influence that was more visual and palpable than ever before. Before the Vietnam War, disaster events that reached national audiences via the media caused feelings of detached horror, such as the Hindenburg disaster, the bombing of Pearl Harbor, or the assassination of John F. Kennedy. In the case of the Kennedy assassination, television news coverage sparked conspiracy theories and brought the reality and finality of death to the fore through an overflow of narrative accounts and journalistic storytelling angles (Yarbrough 1998; see also Davies 2003, 19–21).[2]

Burgeoning technology of the twentieth century complicated collections and their interpretation. As historian Warren Susman notes, American culture "increasingly had to confront the changing forms in which experience was expressed—often rapid change because of technological innovation" (1984, 234). Newer expressive mediums were emerging by the turn of the twentieth century that would take the place of the once-sensationalist newspapers. Newscasts and dramatizations were on the radio, moving images and newsreels entertained Americans at the movie theater, and the introduction of the television additionally contributed to the visual ways in which information was being disseminated, consumed, and subsequently converted into expressive projections of nascent cultural values. The visuality of the television medium, in particular, can be credited with influencing the dynamics of computer-mediated communications and current expectations of information accessibility.

The emotionality of the folk response to disasters that was once represented in the prose of the newspaper medium is now a staple of the communicative exchanges that take place on the Internet. In the past, newspapers would often contain performative rhetoric that encouraged the spread of rumors, legends, and other "unbelievable" tales of gruesomeness. This was particularly true of shocking news stories, such as reports about the exploits of serial killers Jeffrey Dahmer (Tithecott 1997) and Ed Gein (Mitchell 1979). Then, as they do now, folk beliefs about the news stories themselves, as well as the ways that they were reported, made their way into coinciding folkloric texts (see Fine 1992; Fine and Ellis 2010; Langlois 2005). The major difference is that the digital reportage of the news has supplanted print media as the greatest available source for accessing information.

Taking a journalistic viewpoint on the production of humor and folklore in response to media-reported tragedies, folklorist Russell Frank notes that humorous narratives stemming from viewers' observations about the news "may be a response to how that story is told . . . as much as it is a response to the occurrence itself" (2004, 639; see also Brunvand 2001). However, unlike the newspaper and radio outlets that aimed to speak on the people's behalf, new media technology now affords people the opportunity to speak back—and for themselves. The very nature of folklore is predicated on the amalgamation of traditional knowledge through imitation, variation, and innovation. The widespread acceptance of the Internet as a communicative tool has only further demonstrated the behavioral hybridization of face-to-face and virtualized folk processes. Such a merger supports the notion of a "folk" web but, more important, demonstrates how analog and digital hybridization shows users' agency rather than passive consumption.

The Hybridization of Analog and Digital Expressive Behaviors

Communications guru Howard Rheingold proclaims that the "most profoundly transformative potential of connecting human social proclivities to the efficiency of information technology is the chance to do new things together, the potential for cooperating on scales and in ways never before possible" (2003, 114). The Internet medium's amalgamation of analog and digital culture in an imagined space underscores the heterogeneous nature of computer-mediated communications. Numerous people adopt pseudoidentities on the Internet in order to explore fantasies, to protect their reputations in the physical world, or even to enter a state of play with their identity (see Aldred 2010; Booth 2008; Danet 2001; Turkle 1995).

A website or online community where both parties willingly enter may serve as an assumed common ground, although this is not always the case.[3] More important, the connections made online are seen as real and more immediate, and the residual impact of the human desire to connect quickly coalesces around blogs and virtual communities—hardening the influence of symbolic behavior—in ways that the physical world cannot similarly construct without more time to ferment. Essentially, the blurring of public and private spheres online helps to speed along the process of acquiring trust and camaraderie with other people and to circumvent the physical world's usual reluctance to delve into private matters with unfamiliar public audiences. The interpretation of expressive interactions—both by the recipient and the outside observer— are filtered by the contextual differences between the mediums. Ultimately, this results in the hybridization of folklore and vernacular expression.

"Hybridization" refers to the blending of analog and digital forms in the course of their dissemination and enactment. The distinctive characteristics and expressive forms deriving from face-to-face and online realms end up appearing (and being adopted) in *both* expressive venues. As a result, the distinguishing characteristics of each medium are further complicated. Still, it should be stressed that the process of hybridizing folkloric forms is always undertaken and enacted by individuals—either intentionally or outside the realm of their own awareness. Folklorist and communications scholar Robert Glenn Howard defines *hybrid* as an "analytic term referring to a cultural form, expressive behavior, or identity that exhibits features thought to originate from two or more distinct realms" (2010, 682; see also Kapchan 1993; Kapchan and Strong 1999). But what is its social function in the context of the digital age? According to anthropologist Brian Stross, hybridization occurs to "fulfill environmentally sanctioned functions, to fill contextual needs, or to take advantage of opportunities created by new situations. If the environment changes . . . humans seem to devise new forms and formats, . . . with new parameters, new needs, and new opportunities. The hybrid forms that fill new niches in the environment are usually designed, and certainly selected for or against on the basis of their exhibited characteristics, which are usually advantageous over, in this sense superior to, characteristics of either 'parent'" (1999, 261). In other words, hybridization helps people to "catch up" and adapt to the progressing culture by merging the old and familiar with the emergent capabilities of a new medium. An air of authority is attached to hybridized interactions, which also instills a sense of empowerment linked to the notion that hybridization breeds a stronger, superior relationship to (and representation of) expressive behavior than a nonhybridized version.[4]

Social engagement online remains analogous to the dynamics of a neighborhood in the physical world. When participating in a virtual community, the same rules from users' analog lives typically apply when interacting with their digital neighbors—participants seek to cultivate their imagined space and treat it as if it were their own lawn. Like any folk architecture that is built in the physical world, amateur website builders must also use cues from their surroundings and imitate the patterns that they see in order to find a peaceable dwelling for their simulated residency online. Like a "real" neighborhood, a digital one may feature some occupants who get creative with their self-expression. Others may conform to contextually expected notions of presentation. Folk knowledge about web aesthetics becomes the user's default frame of reference to begin their approach to self-presentation online. Those who use site-building templates are not all that different from someone who hires a construction team to build their dream house. And like analog residential properties, the owner of a website is expected to maintain their space or face reprimand or ridicule from the community as being outdated or ignorant. Either way, the motivations that influence aesthetic choices in analog and digital formats are essentially the same. The psychological payoff is similar, with varying levels of exuberance depending on the individual's preference for analog or digital interaction.[5]

Digital interactions usually model, then modify analog modes of expressive interaction. Ultimately, users' success in adapting to the digital medium is reliant on their ability to transpose analog traditions into their digitized persona. Mass media is an outgrowth of modern industrialization, from broadcasting to broadband, and the way that we respond to disaster and tragedy is a reflection of the blending of folk and mass culture over time. While the Internet and mobile communications have not always existed, death and tragedy has accompanied civilization since the beginning. Grieving rituals, collective behavior, and the folk response to emotional stimuli have undergone evolution as contexts have changed. Death, it might be said, is no joke, but facing its actual seriousness through vernacular expression helps people to get by and go forward in their lives. Computer-mediated communication helps to provide such release.

The Normalization of Death in Popular Culture and Mass Media

Throughout American history, the cultural response to disaster or threats of harm has yielded a very strong march toward symbolic gestures that resonate as steps of dealing with the issues at hand. This has taken place in the form of building bomb shelters during the Cold War, donating blood after 9/11, or the Department of Homeland Security's suggestion for homeowners to purchase duct tape in order to be capable of somehow sealing their dwellings from potential toxins out in the surrounding world should a biological attack take place. There is a calming power in these symbolic actions because they project a sense of control over potentially grim or life-ending circumstances.

The overreportage of shocking news is a hallmark of contemporary American mass media. Television networks pull no punches as they vie for prospective viewers' attention, and while some viewers vocalize discontent over the newscasts' emotional blitzkrieg, most clamor for the all-encompassing coverage in the wake of a grievous calamity or scandal (Wenger et al. 1975; Wenger and Friedman 1986). Instead of idly witnessing a news story unfold, motivated participants are now capable of directly influencing how information is disseminated, received, or even subsequently conceptualized by others. And before the newspaper even arrives at the doorstep or the commercial break ends on a news channel, techno-savvy media consumers can now exploit the vast retrieving capabilities of the Internet to find immediate answers for the many probing questions that may be generated in response to a crisis.

From natural disasters and terrorism to the death or falls from grace of a celebrity, new media technology is utilized to provide a forum for public discourse. Global participation in computer-mediated communication continues to grow in our techno-savvy world, and the gruesome realities of many worldwide disasters or disheartening stories are made easily accessible in graphic detail, often with overwhelming statistical, visual, and narrative accompaniment to digest. Naturally, the subject of death has become an increasingly acceptable topic for use in popular culture and casual conversation.

The Latin proverb *Mors Certa, Vita Incerta* translates to "death is certain, life is not." This adage projects a worldview that emphasizes living life to the fullest while downplaying the seriousness of death. In this "spirit," death is now used in the marketing of a commodity or even promoted as a positive, quirky thing. Some tasty desserts are named "death by chocolate" without reproach; a film like *Weekend at Bernie's* (1989) is able to be appreciated for its camp value to mass audiences; earlier, the catchphrase "I ain't afraid of no ghost" from Ray Parker Jr.'s song on the *Ghostbusters* (1984) soundtrack, or Michael Jackson's epic music video *Thriller* (1983), made deathly things something to sing about. Even today, the lead protagonist of the popular Showtime television series *Dexter* is a serial killer whom the audience cheers on instead of shuns. Video games like the *Grand Theft Auto* franchise glorify the opportunity to mercilessly beat and kill random people in urban environments (see Miller 2008). And yet playing these games or enjoying fictional shows that casually depict death or violence is not necessarily a warning sign of sociopathic tendencies but rather an indicator of a mind at play.[6] The same suspension of emotion and reasoning that is tapped while enjoying these activities is also used as a defense mechanism in times of peril (see Bryant 2003). Humor and other forms of vernacular expression serve as ammunition for the outward expression of creativity.

Death and tragedy conjure up a lot of different emotions for most people. Analog precedents abound for the folk response to tragedy, but the burgeoning patterns of online behavior have been rapidly accumulating since the 1990s and especially following the terrorist attacks of September 11, 2001. Without a doubt, avoiding the social and psychological impact of the unwavering graphic nature of the news is nearly impossible. In essence, the Internet invites participation—especially following a traumatic event—because there are fewer outlets for psychological release or symbolic gesturing in the physical world owing to greater opportunities for self-entertainment via new media.

At first glance the mockery of death through vernacular expression may appear to be a counterintuitive strategy for quelling internal anxiety following a tragic event. On the other hand, symbolic expression serves to make seemingly inappropriate topics of conversation into pleasurable ones—a major function of humorous expression.[7] Engaging in the telling or enjoyment of death humor creates a rhetorical sense of defiance (and even denial) against the bonds of our inevitable mortality. And more important, the humorous responses, personal narratives, and material productions that emerge in the wake of disaster are engendered with answers about the ways that people respond to highly stressful situations through folklore. But what role has the media played in catalyzing this emergence of death into the anxiety-laden folkloric expressions that follow disasters today?

The aura of death was greatly diluted by the prolonged and incessantly graphic media coverage of the Vietnam War, which effectively neutered the emotional impact of death by desensitizing viewers to its occurrence (see Kearl 1989, 385). It is therefore unsurprising, notes Christie Davies, that disaster jokes "did not exist in substantial numbers, and indeed probably did not exist at all, before the rise of television" (2003, 16). Media coverage brought the tragedy of death into our living rooms in ways that the print reports of World War I or the newsreels of World War II could not. The disconnect between the images on the screen and the viewers at home created a mental buffer. A sense of cognitive delusion helped to facilitate a continued dissociation between the real finality of death and the individual's own perception of mortality. Accordingly, death themes became more widely adopted into mainstream folklore repertoires in order to mock or defuse the anxieties associated with its presence. This is not to say that death was wholly avoided in the public discourse before the Vietnam era; it was simply more acceptable to openly discuss or mock in subsequent years as a symptom of the media's chronicling of the war. This has been interpreted by some scholars who note the popularity of the era's emergent "dead baby" jokes that coincided with the legalization of abortions in the United States (Dundes 1979), or the "Auschwitz" jokes that emerged following the airing of the popular 1978 television miniseries *The Holocaust*, which dramatized the struggles of a Jewish family as they struggled to endure Nazi oppression and extermination (Dundes and Hauschild 1983; see also Barrick 1980; Dundes 1987a; Linke and Dundes 1988; Oring 1983).[8]

As a consequence of the mass media's normalization of death and dismemberment during the Vietnam era, we now conceptualize "real" tragedies in the way that we are best equipped to relate: through our own extensive cultural inventories that are informed by folk and popular culture. Once the façade of death denial begins to crumble—such as when a disaster strikes and we are not permitted to dismiss its realness through rhetoric—people converge in meaningfully symbolic ways in order to make sense of their shifting emotions and sense of grounding in the world. And when an actual disaster or tragedy is at hand, humor and narratives that connect to others' experience are shared in order to demonstrate communal solidarity or to temper the emotionality of the event. Nevertheless, it bears noting that people have acquired the means to express themselves via technology long before the emergence of Web 2.0, yet often in ways that share many of the same attributes as the jokes, narratives, and software-edited (or "Photoshopped") artwork seen circulating online today.[9]

The fear of imminent death is composed of six distinguishing features: fears of dependency or loss of control; isolation and loneliness; pain; physical disfigurement; loss of dignity; and the unknown (Kearl 1989, 487–88). Denial is carried out by symbolic actions and interactions, both through narrative discourse and, most visibly, through attempts at problem solving. Rejecting the seriousness of death does not necessarily require a blatant dismissal of an event's realness. The process of displacement compensates for the disturbing quality of death by drawing individuals into other activities or symbolic actions (such as kneading dough, or carving wood, or even compiling an oral history) that are often found to be soothing or therapeutic by mourners. In alleviating the emotional weight of death, the Internet enables the perpetuation of cognitive denial in that its simulative liminality helps to suspend the full force of reality. Because we feel truly connected to our digital expressions, we can also take a small bit of comfort in knowing that (beyond computer viruses and electrical outages at home) we are still here; we are still connected to our fellow humans.

So what do these shifting currents of expressive behavior in the response to disaster mean, and how are they influenced by folklore? More important, why do they matter? To fully demonstrate the traditionality of contemporary digital folklore, it is imperative to closely scrutinize the telecommunicated modes of symbolic expression that preceded the widespread adoption of the Internet as a communicative tool. Furthermore, it is necessary to consider the historical contexts of several noteworthy events that influenced the dissemination of folkloric materials via pre-Internet technology in order to identify comparable expressive motifs between the past and the present. These factors help to demonstrate the power of repetition and variation, even across different expressive mediums over time. As the next chapter shows, they provide a comparative baseline of mass-mediated disasters from before the digital age and connote the traditionality of contemporary hybridized folklore.

CHAPTER 2

❧

Changing Technologies, Changing Tastes

THE EVOLUTION OF HUMOR AND MASS-MEDIATED DISASTERS
IN THE LATE TWENTIETH CENTURY

The Three Mile Island accident and NASA's Challenger space shuttle disaster are among the two most notable catastrophes to occur in the United States between the end of the media-saturated Vietnam era and the emergence and popular adoption of Internet technology. By comparison, the highly visualized and narrative responses found online in the ensuing days and months after the terrorist attacks of September 11, 2001, reveal correlative traditions that suggest a linking influence of the mass media in the folk response to disaster. In building off the previous chapter, I would like to provide a historical reference point for understanding the evolution of contemporary disaster responses through an overview of the regional and widespread circulation of humor, photocopylore, and material culture in the folk responses to the Three Mile Island accident of 1979 and the "sick" joke cycle that followed the Challenger disaster of 1986, one of the first mass-mediated disasters to be extensively studied by folklorists (Ellis 1991; Oring 1987; Simons 1986; Smyth 1986).

Pre-Internet Responses to Tragedy:
The Three Mile Island Accident

For many people today, the initialism "TMI" stands for "too much information." For the people of central Pennsylvania, the letters have stood for something else: Three Mile Island. Beyond the TMI initialism lies a greater symbolic meaning for central Pennsylvanians, one that oozes a multitude of emotions in response to the memories and subsequent folk responses to the near-catastrophic accident at the nuclear power plant that took place on March 28, 1979. The story of the partial core meltdown at Three Mile Island is both a cautionary tale and an intriguing, comparative example of how journalists

26

and regular people responded to the threat of obliteration before the instantaneity of Internet communication was available and underscores the former limitations that surrounded the dissemination of regional folklore.

The United States was in difficult economic times during the late 1970s. As a result of a global fuel shortage, oil prices had risen from $3 to $30 per barrel in just under seven years (Ivory 2007, 133). In an effort to curb American dependency on foreign oil and to promote autonomous energy production domestically, pundits hailed nuclear energy as the latest, greatest, and cheapest means for solving America's energy crisis. Construction on the Three Mile Island (often referred to as TMI) nuclear plant began in September 1974. At its opening in December 1978, Three Mile Island was considered to be a state-of-the-art facility. Despite a sharp debate throughout the country over the safety and viability of nuclear energy, many local residents expressed optimism at central Pennsylvania's leap into the future (Leppzer 1980, 62–65).

At 4:00 a.m. on the morning of March 28, 1979, a series of mechanical and human errors resulted in a partial meltdown of the Unit 2 pressurized reactor at the Three Mile Island nuclear facility near Harrisburg, Pennsylvania (Walker 2006). The infamous accident took place less than five months after Three Mile Island began commercial operations—forever altering the region's view of nuclear energy and government bureaucracy. The company that operated the plant, Metropolitan Edison, excelled at mishandling all public relations and flustered the public during a series of tense, uninformative, and fabricated press conferences. Peoples' trust in technology, government, and the media were understandably shaken. In an effort to circumvent and thwart the continued influence of corporate entities in their personal lives, folklore emerged as a means of relieving the tremendous tensions surrounding the region. While the uncertain situation was ultimately remedied through intervention from the federal government, the events and aftermath of the accident at Three Mile Island served as perfect breeding grounds for folkloric production and dissemination. In what was the greatest nuclear disaster in the history of the United States, the Three Mile Island accident came to symbolize the heated debate over the safety of nuclear energy that weighed so heavily on the minds of many Americans at the time.

As with many major headlines, reporters descended on the areas surrounding Three Mile Island immediately after the story broke. Information was hard to come by, and local officials were wrestling with ways to curb panic while seeking a way to prevent nuclear meltdown. As the story unfolded, news coverage and public awareness became inescapable, especially for those residing in central Pennsylvania. While early news reports from Three Mile Island were "concerned with describing the extent of the radiation venting, the degree of danger resulting from exposure to it, and what went wrong in the first place," the media's focus quickly shifted to the emotional stress of individuals living within a twenty-five-mile radius of the plant as the crisis lingered on without resolution (Fischer 1994, 27).

The residents of areas surrounding Three Mile Island referenced their cultural inventory in order to process the events that were unfolding around them, including the foreign intrusion of the media, random "experts," and curious gawkers who drifted into town. American studies scholar Lonna Malmsheimer notes that people responded to Three Mile Island by conceptualizing and interpreting the chaos around them in fantastical terms, with specific correlations drawn to popular culture such as television and especially motion pictures:

> Many informants reported a wide-ranging search for analogies. In this search the individual sorted through the cultural inventory of experience, both actual and vicarious, both historical and fictive, as if these various models of thought and behavior were of the same kind in terms of their relevance and reliability. . . . Such "loose" thinking is a continuous source of creative adaptation and is also *characteristic of the mind at play.* . . . Science fictions and images, historical narrative and images, and previous actual experiences came to mind and were used in attempts to *normalize the situation.* (Malmsheimer 1986, 38, emphasis added)

In Middletown, Pennsylvania—one of the boroughs in close proximity to Three Mile Island—the lone movie theater in town (which runs only one film at a time) happened to be showing *The China Syndrome*, which portrays the chilling consequences of a nuclear plant meltdown (Del Tredici 1980). Coincidentally, the film had been released in theaters less than two weeks before the accident occurred. Needless to say, popular culture was poised to be included in the folkloric "fallout" from Three Mile Island.

To be sure, our cultural inventories are made up of images that symbolically encapsulate an idea or event; these images are drawn from our interaction with mass-mediated information and visual data. In the case of Three Mile Island, there was considerable imagery associated with nuclear energy going wrong, and it clearly fueled the folk response. In the absence of information or symbolic communal solidarity, people turned to their cultural inventories for guidance, which led directly to a particularly salient symbol: a nuclear mushroom cloud.

According to historian Robert Lifton, the images of destruction stemming from the bombing of Hiroshima and Nagasaki during World War II directly inform the modern consciousness by permeating traditional boundaries of destruction and eroding conventions of literal or metaphorical immortality (Lifton 1968, 1969, 1970, 1979, 1982). The crisis at Three Mile Island not only invoked the destructive imagery of Hiroshima but also "forced individuals to remember the bombing . . . and led them to confront, if not resolve, their fears of human extinction and the destruction of all nature" (Malmsheimer 1986, 40). Indeed, as false rumors spread of a hydrogen bubble forming inside one of the cooling towers during the crisis, many people reported imagining visions of an atomic mushroom cloud, even though it was a scientific impossibility. Before long, photocopylore emerged to reflect these concerns.

Generally speaking, Xerox- or photocopylore was meant to be used for rhetorically countering the propriety of corporate environments through the use of anonymously circulated materials that often lampooned the rigors of being an employee or joked about taboo subjects like race, gender, and sex (see Dundes and Pagter [1975] 1978, 1987, 1991b, 1996, 2000; Hatch and Jones 1997; Michael 1995; Preston 1974, 1994; Roemer 1994).[1] Copy and fax machines were used to duplicate and/or send these hand-drawn, amateurish materials before they were posted on the individual walls or communal bulletin boards of a workplace. The content was sometimes graphic and crude but was nevertheless meant to elicit laughter or amusement in a restrictive social setting. The anonymity of the texts' original creator removed accountability, and because they bypassed social restrictions of expected "professional" decorum, humorous texts could be displayed or passed along from one individual to another at the office without reproach.

To be sure, photocopied humor was in modest circulation during and after the Three Mile Island accident, and many materials poked fun at the incompetency of Metropolitan Edison and their handling of the accident, as well as wordplay and humor about the destruction of nearby land (see fig. 2). However, the most prevalent means of vernacular expression among residents of the area (outside of sharing jokes, rumors, and personal experience narratives) could be seen in the creation of unique T-shirts, artifacts,[2] games, and other ephemera (see figs. 3–5).[3]

During and after the Three Mile Island accident, people had access to communication technology that connected them with others, but as regional folklorists noted, many of the circulating jokes or narratives did not usually leave the region (Kassovic 1981).[4] Among the most popular in circulation were:

Q: What's the five-day forecast for Harrisburg, Pennsylvania?
A: Two days.
[Variations also added "with temperatures reaching 3000 degrees"[5] or "Cloudy with a 40% chance of survival."]

Q: What melts on the ground, but not in your hand?
A: Hershey, Pennsylvania. [The location of the Hershey chocolate factory.]

Q: What does TMI stand for?
A: Too Many Idiots.

FOR SALE

RECREATIONAL PROPERTY

This unique *PRIVATE ISLAND* on the Susquehanna River offers:

- FENCED IN ACREAGE approximately THREE MILES in length.
- ACCESS by MODERN BRIDGE.
- CLOSE to SCHOOLS, CHURCHES, HOSPITALS, AIRPORT, GOLF COURSE, and STATE CAPITAL.
- RADIANT HEAT
- TOTAL ELECTRIC LIVING — Includes own electrical generators (one operable...the other needs work)
- MAID SERVICE at the touch of a button (Remote Control Robot)

This NATIONALLY KNOWN LANDMARK, visited by PRESIDENT CARTER, is being *SACRIFICED* by owner for health reasons.

CALL NOW!   HOT BARGAIN!   WON'T LAST LONG!

PHONE: M. Edison, 944-3902, Middletown, PA.

Figure 2. This mock advertisement, an example of photocopylore following the Three Mile Island nuclear accident, was found in circulation on November 28, 1988. Courtesy of the Archives of Folklore and Ethnography, Penn State Harrisburg.

Figure 3. A T-shirt created during a Dickinson College (Carlisle, PA) design competition reads: "Squeeze Me, I Radiate / Kiss Me, I Meltdown: 3 Mile Island / Middletown, PA." Courtesy of the Archives of Folklore and Ethnography, Penn State Harrisburg.

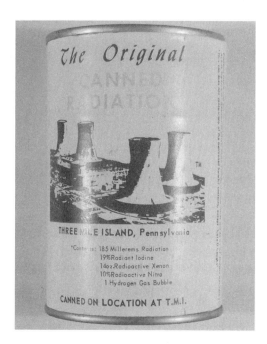

Figure 4. "Canned Radiation," an example of locally created Three Mile Island ephemera, could be purchased as a gag gift at general stores within a thirty-mile radius of the nuclear reactor following the accident. Courtesy of the Archives of Folklore and Ethnography, Penn State Harrisburg.

Figure 5. *React-or: A Radiating Experience*, a Monopoly-like, Three Mile Island–themed board game, was created by central Pennsylvania residents Adam, Diane, and Edward Sandnes in the summer of 1979. Courtesy of the Archives of Folklore and Ethnography, Penn State Harrisburg.

Many of the jokes play on the proximity of other towns within a short radius of Harrisburg, or hint at embitterment against Metropolitan Edison. Indeed, Metropolitan Edison's suspicious determination to keep internal matters under wraps led some to believe that they were fabricating their risk assessments or blatantly covering up reportage of their incompetency. This speculative mistrust only further heightened individuals' own anxieties, which they ultimately projected in many of the personal narratives and rumors that surfaced as the crisis was resolved.

In lieu of being at the scene of an accident or natural disaster, people must rely on the reportage of others to define their perceptions of the event. If high standards for accuracy are not met, rumormongering and other folkloric creations can be expected to fill in the blanks as fact (see Fine and Ellis 2010). To a great extent, the media's coverage of the Three Mile Island accident— which at times consisted of speculation, misinformation, and the regurgitation of unverified rumors (presented as "the concerns of individuals living in the area") amid the chaos and uncertainty—played a significant role in perpetuating an environment of fear and discontent during the crisis (Nimmo and Combs 1985, 60–86). In particular, the media's effect lingered on the minds of local residents in the months following the Three Mile Island accident.

Among the people of the Harrisburg metropolitan area, the lack of verifiable information served as ideal breeding grounds for rumor diffusion and great uncertainty about their health and well-being, as well as their community's health. Many people reported having nightmares or extreme spikes of anxiety over the possible side effects of radiation exposure in the aftermath of the Three Mile Island accident (Leppzer 1980, 12–16, 21–50). News of animal mutations and deaths, record levels of abortions at Harrisburg area hospitals, and increased instances of cancer abounded (Del Tredici 1980; Leppzer 1980). People reported greater instances of animal mutations and deaths, human abortions, and cancer cases because *that was the expected result of exposure to radiation.* Apocalyptic films like *The Day After* (1983) and other popular media helped to enhance the reality of this fiction and served as a folkloric conduit.

Today, when a tragedy penetrates national news coverage—even for a brief period—regional folklore does not remain regional. A vast network of bloggers, commentators, unaffiliated participants, and journalists descends on stories, extracts and comments, and ultimately archives them all over the Internet, where they remain until they are deleted by a site administrator, if ever. When the Three Mile Island accident left the national spotlight and returned to being an exclusively regional news story, the events only remained palpable and salient in regional folklore circles. This simply does not happen anymore.[6]

Meaningful community interaction and symbolic unity was difficult to establish amid the misinformation, confusion, and general uncertainty that loomed over the situation at Three Mile Island. To cope with the anxiety, residents near Three Mile Island looked inward in order to create an outward expression of creativity. Taken collectively with the oral narratives, circulating jokes, or other parodic artwork found among groups of people, Three Mile Island folklore clearly demonstrates the same transmission patterns and traditional expressive modes as materials found in contemporary circulation. The elements of structure, calculated intent, and purposeful dissemination are of the same ilk and suggest a connecting lineage between past and present material. In many ways, these fax and photocopied texts strongly resemble the visual intentions and distribution patterns of today's Photoshopped humor, which not only suggests traditionality but further supports the notion that technology stimulates—and does *not* diminish—folkloric expression.[7]

The Challenger Disaster Joke Cycle

On the morning of January 28, 1986, the National Aeronautics and Space Administration (NASA) approved the launch of the Challenger space shuttle, despite unfavorable weather conditions at the Kennedy Space Center near Cape Canaveral, Florida. Shortly after liftoff, the space shuttle exploded in the air, killing all seven of the Challenger's crew members. Among them was civilian Christa McAuliffe, who was slated to become the first teacher in space. Adding to the shock and consternation of the fatal explosion was the fact that the accident was broadcast live on CNN and was being shown at countless schools across the United States in recognition of McAuliffe's involvement with NASA's "Teacher in Space Project." When the space shuttle exploded, communications scholars estimated that news of the accident had disseminated faster than any other American news event since the deaths of Presidents Franklin Delano Roosevelt and John F. Kennedy—and the troubling reality was that more children than adults may have witnessed the event while at school that day (Wright et al. 1989, 27).

Although the Three Mile Island accident garnered national coverage in the media, the greatest concentration of both news coverage and vernacular discourse, including humor, took place regionally.[8] On the contrary, the "Challenger disaster," as the accident came to be known, received continuous coverage in the national news media for months following the accident. The event, and its subsequent narration in the media, made it a public tragedy; beyond the immediate grief surrounding the loss of life and the longing for answers to the cause of the explosion, there was also the shattering of the prideful perception for many that NASA was "one of the few American bureaucracies that worked—that got the job done" (Oring 1987, 281–82; see also Simons 1986, 261–62, 271).

Because the space shuttle explosion happened on live television, the tragedy, however gruesome, was nevertheless "speakable" and "viewable," in the journalistic sense. Video and images of the event could be played and replayed, and they were. Within a matter of weeks, following a brief latency period (Ellis 1991, 112), a number of "sick" jokes about the event appeared, and they circulated widely for over three months.[9] The jokes were an act of rebellion against the media's coverage of the event, with sordid punchlines aimed at the "unspeakable" dimensions of the tragedy. Although crude, they were not intended to be hostile against the victims but rather to highlight the "psychically significant theme[s] underlying the jokes," such as death, dismemberment, or mutilation (Smyth 1986, 252–53). For instance, in the disaster's ensuing media coverage, Christa McAuliffe's death attracted the most attention because of her nonastronaut status and largely symbolic, nontechnical role in the shuttle mission. Expectedly, McAuliffe was also the lone crewmember to be singled out in joke cycles by name while the "other astronauts" faded into generic anonymity. The rhetoric behind many of the Challenger jokes was aimed at capitalizing on the media's focus on McAuliffe.[10] However, they additionally connote an acknowledgment of the fact that she was "one of us"—a civilian—and that her placement on the mission was a foolhardy attempt for publicity, not astronautic ingenuity. Many of these jokes included elements of wordplay and double entendres (predominantly using the organization of a riddle formula):

Q: What color were Christa McAuliffe's eyes?
A: Blue. One blew this way, one blew that way.[11]

Q: What was the last thing Christa McAuliffe told her husband when she left for Florida?
A: You feed the dog, I'll feed the fish.

Q: What were Christa McAuliffe's last words?
A: What's this red button for?

Q: What was the last thing to go through Christa McAuliffe's mind?
A: The control panel.
[Variations: The fuselage; her asshole, etc.]

Note that many of the jokes even play with the finality of death by drawing attention to the "last" words and actions of McAuliffe and the other astronauts onboard (Ellis 1991; Oring 1987, 283).[12] While their tenor appears quite hostile, these jokes and their targets were meant to be playful, counterhegemonic gestures against the media's narration of the tragedy and not openly hostile against the victims themselves. Indeed, many forms of humor (including those pertaining to race, ethnicity, or regional/national identity) do not arise out of aggression, conflict, or threat, but for playful purposes (Davies 2002, 2011). Joke tellers did not openly hate Christa McAuliffe, nor were they intending to seriously mock or belittle the death of the crew. McAuliffe just happened to be an especially recognizable figure because of the media's excessive reportage (paying special attention to her) and thus became a more common target in the joke cycle. Of course, some jokes targeted the failures of NASA:

Q: What does NASA stand for?
A: Need another seven astronauts.
[Variation: Now accepting seven applications.]

While others incorporated commercial products to land a reaction:

Q: Why do they drink Pepsi at NASA?
A: Because they can't get 7-Up!

Q: What was the cause of the Challenger explosion?
A: The crew was free-basing Tang!

Q: How did they know Christa McAuliffe had dandruff?
A: Her "head and shoulders" washed up on shore.[13]

Q: What was the last thing said on the Challenger?
A: I want a light . . . No, I meant a Bud Light!

It is important to note the infusion of commercial products into the punch line of several jokes about the Challenger disaster because they further underscore joke tellers' awareness of the mass media and its role in their cultural inventories. These jokes are significant in that "the cause of the tragedy is reduced to being compared to or part of a television commercial" (Smyth 1986, 258). 7-Up is a popular soft drink, Tang is a fruit-flavored drink that is often associated with the U.S. space program, Head and Shoulders is a popular shampoo product, and Bud Light is a popular domestic beer. All of these products were typically brought to individuals' attention via mass media out-lets. For example, in order to "get" the Bud Light joke's punch line, one must be able to recall (from their cultural inventory) the popular "Gimme a Light" Budweiser commercials from 1986–87 in which a bar or restaurant patron asks for a "light" and is presented with some literal-meaning illuminated object that is not a beer, to which they clarify that they wanted a Bud Light beer instead.[14] Of course, this contextual information also speaks to the ephemerality of some topical humor. These kinds of disaster jokes and fantastical narratives helped individuals "put disasters back where they are usually seen: in fiction and pop-ular culture" (Kuipers 2011, 41).

Like the humor stemming from other mass-mediated disasters, most (if not all) of the Challenger jokes were rhetorically aimed at the media's attempt to influence viewers' emotional sentiments and interpretations of the explo-sion. By sharing Challenger disaster humor, joke tellers (and listeners) tapped into their cultural inventories to encode and decode intricate bits of rhetoric about popular culture, consumerism, and knowledge about the news event itself. Their navigation of this cultural inventory, juxtaposed with a desire to control the narrative power of a mass-mediated disaster, yielded colorful col-lections at the time of the explosion. However, the lasting impact of these materials was (and continues to be) their influence on subsequent joke cycles by further encouraging people to mock death and rhetorically chastise the role of the media in our understanding of a tragic event.

But beyond humor, the spirit of these joke cycles—namely their function as a rhetorical counter to the mass media's emotionally hegemonic reportage of a death, disaster, or shocking, contentious event—found a welcome home on the emergent World Wide Web in the late 1980s and early 1990s and helped make the medium thrive while also cultivating a new form of expressive cul-ture. As the next chapter shows, Web 1.0 and eventually Web 2.0 expressive interfaces transmitted a wealth of materials evolving from the traditions that came to light during the Challenger disaster.

CHAPTER 3

❧

From 9/11 to the
Death of bin Laden

VERNACULAR EXPRESSION AND THE
EMERGENCE OF WEB 2.0

Dialing Up Web 1.0: The Emergent Internet
(before 9/11 "Changed Everything")

Unquestionably, the early 1990s were a crucial time in the Internet's development as a communications powerhouse. This was the Web 1.0 era, where connections to the Internet were typically made through a dial-up service with 56k bandwidth (versus today's broadband Internet accessibility and the current global average Internet speed of 1.7 megabytes per second).[1] Websites were largely static, instead of dynamic or interactive; many sites were set up as "read-only," which inherently prohibited users from modifying or directly contributing anything. Amateur personal webpages[2] frequently showcased "frames" and other common aesthetic cues, such as the incorporation of a "guestbook" for visitors, or the display of a "webring" that provided hyperlinks to several other sites with similar content.[3] Naturally, these examples magnify the stark differences between past and present iterations of the World Wide Web.[4]

The popularization of the World Wide Web during the 1990s carried the traditions and patterns of photocopylore and oral/face-to-face forms of vernacular expression right into the emergent online medium. The familiar elements of traditional letter writing and other basic communication conventions were being adopted into the most popular expressive venues of the burgeoning World Wide Web—e-mail, chat rooms (notably Internet Relay Chat or IRC), discussion groups, lists, multiuser dungeons (MUDs), virtual communities, ASCII art, and personal webpages (Danet 2001; see also Kirshenblatt-Gimblett 1996; Rheingold 2000). And while early interactions may have especially taken advantage of the luxury of anonymity to assume fantastical roles or to test the limits of taste while joking (see Ellis 2003), the emergence of Web 2.0 diminished the attraction of such proclivities.

Observing the early folkloric qualities of computer-generated and mediated materials, folklorist Paul Smith (1991) remarked that "with the folk uses of the computer, people rarely stray from the application of word-processing and simple graphics. They may tinker with the texts and images, but their main aim is to encapsulate and disseminate such items" (276; see also Bronner 2012). Indeed, a certain degree of technical skill was required to fully participate in the creation and (especially) dissemination of computerized folklore; moreover, certain professions required the use of such technologies, while many others did not, which made these materials rather esoteric and more difficult to identify as "folk." In a relatively short amount of time, though, a basic mastery of the personal computer's interface and the more widespread ability to access the World Wide Web became commonplace for many Americans. By the year 2000, more people were actively *participating* in online activities rather than simply collecting and/or disseminating material as in years past. Learning how to interact with computers (for a variety of reasons, from composing letters to creating art) became a part of children's socialization.

As the burgeoning Internet forum took shape and users worked to configure adequate means of adopting and/or transmitting folklore and expressive patterns from face-to-face communication, wholly new patterns of folk culture—native to the World Wide Web—emerged as well. In time, the context of whether an item was first transmitted online or in "the real world" also became increasingly difficult to distinguish.[5] Drawing on the cues and *content* (in many cases) from oral tradition and face-to-face communications, mass-mediated disasters became easier and easier to comment upon online—and often in unique and creative ways, despite the early Internet's text-heavy presentation and rather basic aesthetic composition.

Archived examples of online forum discussions, jokes, and opinion posts about the current events of the Web 1.0 era are still available online in some cases. Importantly, they reveal early folk experimentations with performing and sharing humorous narratives online, predominantly through e-mail circulation, on personal webpages, or through various newsgroups and online discussion forums. Ultimately, these expressive outlets were used to facilitate the dissemination of the folk responses to newsworthy events such as the bloody siege of the Branch Davidian religious compound in Waco, Texas, in 1993; the contentious verdict of "not guilty" in the O. J. Simpson murder trial in 1995;[6] the untimely death of Princess Diana in 1997;[7] and the gruesome Columbine massacre in Littleton, Colorado, on April 20, 1999,[8] among others.[9] Much like the ever-influential Challenger disaster joke cycle, the humorous materials from the Web 1.0 era remain relevant and important today, as evidenced by their continued incorporation into contemporary joke formulations and other folkloric motifs through repetition and variation—regardless as to whether or not a joke teller is aware of such influence.

The new convenience and greater access to information on the Internet turned the mass media into a double-edged sword following a catastrophe. By providing large quantities of information in a short amount of time—coupled with the ability to hasten its transmission from person to person with tremendous ease—the Internet allowed for a chainlike reaction of information dispersal to occur in the event of a major news event (see Blank 2007). With this in mind, it should not be surprising to note that fewer than fifty jokes regarding the Challenger space shuttle disaster were recorded at the time of its occurrence (Oring 1992; Smyth 1986), whereas over one hundred and fifty O. J. Simpson jokes about the alleged murder of his spouse and her boyfriend emerged as the Internet began to take off as an accepted medium for folkloric transmission in the mid-1990s (Lamb 1994); and over three hundred jokes about the death of Princess Diana surfaced in 1997 and 1998, owing in large part to the growing accessibility, convenience, and popularity of the World Wide Web (Davies 2003, 29).

While the interface of the Web 1.0 Internet was heavily text oriented and aesthetically limited, it nevertheless established a foundation for the more advanced and sophisticated expressive features of the Web 2.0 era. Popularized as a term by media mogul Tim O'Reilly in 2004 and later adopted by Internet users and scholars worldwide, the emergence of "Web 2.0" marked a major shift in the expressive culture of the Internet toward the highly visual, interactive, and streamlined (see O'Reilly 2005). Supplanting Web 1.0's diminished opportunities for dynamic interaction and largely text-heavy presentation, the Web 2.0 era has come to welcome new traditions of user-manipulated artwork, Flash video capabilities, and user-uploaded videos to YouTube (with its dual ability to act as a source of entertainment and a tool for expression) as well as weblogs and blogging, social networking, and various other intricate means of communicating and symbolically mingling with peers online. A key component to emphasize, though, is the noticeable shift in the emphasis from text-based material to a more visually expressive culture (see Blank 2012; Hathaway 2005; Kuipers 2005).

When it comes to interpreting the news, as Russell Frank notes, "image can overpower text" (2011, 20). Thus, in the course of cognitively processing the implications or metaphorical "weight" that may be associated with a death, disaster, or shocking event (be it individually, locally, or in broader, even national or global, terms), it is no surprise that highly visual and aesthetic forms of expressive humor have become increasingly utilized for vernacular expression since the arrival of the Web 2.0 era. Just as photocopylore provided visualized renderings of folk humor, the Internet has facilitated the rapid dissemination of a distinct expressive proclivity in the form of user-manipulated art, better known as "Photoshopped" art.

The popular emergence of Photoshopping for comedic purposes (instead of personal or professional photo editing) really began to pick up steam as individuals explored its symbolic expressive potential while responding online to the first attack on American soil since the bombing of Pearl Harbor in 1941: the terrorist attacks of September 11, 2001. And although various kinds of folklore emerged online in the wake of 9/11—many of them clearly traditional and widely disseminated online,[10] especially via e-mail—I would like to pay particular attention to the *visual* component of circulating Photoshopped humor, as these materials represent the earliest and most salient expressive forays into the burgeoning Web 2.0 era. Additionally, they preview the eventual trajectory of folk culture in the digital age toward greater visuality in vernacular expression as the online medium continued to develop.

9/11 and Thereafter: Patterns of Expression in the Virtual Folk Response to Disaster

I was all of seventeen years old when the terrorist attacks of September 11, 2001, took place. It is a day that is forever etched into my memory. I remember that clear, blue Tuesday morning like it was yesterday: having manipulated my guidance counselor into allowing me to take a breezy "consumer math" class during my senior year of high school—a class that taught sleepy or unmotivated twelfth graders how to balance a checkbook instead of rousing them to find the value of X in any given scenario—I remember going over the eccentricities of calculating a tip when an announcement came over the school's PA system around 9:30 a.m. With a calm, monotone delivery, the principal stated that terrorists had hijacked several planes and crashed them into the Twin Towers and the Pentagon. Our teacher tried in vain to bring the class back to the lesson at hand, but everyone else was more concerned with finding out what had happened. In an instant, it seemed, the world had changed before our very eyes.

I grew up in Damascus, Maryland, a suburb of Washington, DC, and the news of an attack taking place in two of the Eastern Seaboard's most vibrant economic and political hubs (in addition to the close distance of the attacks to our families and personal lives) made the disaster all the more palpable to everyone taking in the news as it unfolded. In the halls of my own high school, in the moments following the announcement of the attacks I witnessed not only displays of grief, fear, or anger but also, and most predominantly, humor. As we were being quickly bused home because of safety concerns, I heard a gruff student yell at one of my peers of Saudi Arabian descent, "Hey, tell your uncles 'thanks' for getting us out of school early," followed by a chorus of chuckles—and this was before we even knew who was responsible for the attacks or what had even happened in full. "Looks like we're gonna smoke us some camels, boys," remarked another, invoking—perhaps subconsciously—the previously circulating folk humor collected during the Gulf War (see Dundes and Pagter 1991a).

Like so many others, I turned to the television for answers. Following a less-than-comforting declaration by President George W. Bush that the United States had been attacked by a "faceless coward," new details started to trickle in. My shift at a local grocery store began at 3:00 p.m. that day, and I watched as many Washingtonians who lived in my community came to buy up supplies and morosely walk about with a thousand-mile stare. "The end is near," one man grimly uttered to me during checkout. "You better get right with God, son. There might not be much time left." Others pointed out the deafening silence in the sky. I remember looking up and not seeing a single plane in flight for the first time in my life. Looking past the ripples in the clouds, I could sense the tension in the air as my neighbors quietly awaited answers for questions that had yet to form.

In addition to the iconic visual markers that were branded onto the public's consciousness during subsequent media reportage, my recollection of 9/11 is quite vivid and personalized. I clearly remember the inflection of voices that I heard, the colors that I saw, the emotions that I felt, the people whom I encountered, the things that were said, and of course the linear progression of the day itself. However, the ability to recall the nuances of my day on 9/11 is not a unique gift. These recollections are examples of "flashbulb memories," which—very much like a camera—vividly capture the visual, aural, and other sensitive elements of an individual's whereabouts and their subsequent actions as they coincide with (and respond to) a significant historical moment (Brown and Kulick 1977). As a major event unfolds, the capturing and storage of flashbulb memories is triggered by intersecting elements of surprise, emotional intensity, and the perception of consequentiality, or how the event will impact history (Kirshenblatt-Gimblett 2003; see also Hathaway 2005). For example, many people can vividly recall exactly what they were doing and how they felt when they learned that President John F. Kennedy had been assassinated in

1963 (Wolfenstein and Kliman 1965) or when the Challenger space shuttle exploded (Ellis 1991; Smyth 1986).

In the days and months following 9/11, American media coverage of the aftermath aired around the clock as the era welcomed unprecedented, uninterrupted twenty-four-hour news coverage that influenced how the event was interpreted by average viewers. On television and online, image after grisly image was repeatedly shown from new angles; side shots of personal narratives from the scene abounded; images of planes striking the Twin Towers and footage of people running for their lives or jumping to their deaths filled the screen. Viewers were forced to rewitness the horror over and over again, making the tension feel every bit as impactful in locations far from the scenes of disaster as it was for those living near them (see Blank 2009c). The bombardment of the ensuing news reportage, coupled with high anxiety over the looming confusion, significantly influenced the folklore that would emerge from the ashes of the World Trade Center, the Pentagon, and United Airlines Flight 93.[11]

We heard the phrase in the media, we heard it from government leaders, and eventually we heard it in folk and popular culture alike: "9/11 changed everything." After the terrorist attacks of September 11, the popular consensus was that "humor is dead" and that joking was no longer allowed (see Gournelos and Greene 2011). Late-night comedians like David Letterman and Jay Leno were cautious about returning to the air with their shows. *Saturday Night Live*, a New York comedy standard since 1975, returned to broadcast a few weeks after 9/11 with a somber tone, which was finally broken by the opening dialogue between SNL producer Lorne Michaels (who asked, "Can we be funny?") and New York City mayor Rudy Giuliani (who replied, "Why start now?"), all of which served as a symbolic gesture that it was indeed "okay to laugh" again. Irreverent cartoons like *South Park* and satirical programs like *The Daily Show with Jon Stewart* also returned from hiatus after several weeks passed without further incident. But while these shows resumed their artistic deployment of humor, many jokes were already in circulation—saying what couldn't be said in institutional settings, such as television or radio broadcasts. Indeed, as Christie Davies observes, "Television is hegemonic, the Internet libertarian" (2003, 30). And so the Internet took over as a means of communicating humor in these times of social uneasiness and decorum.

Hungarian ethnologist Lajos Csaszi asserts that after 9/11, the Internet "provided a public space that was distinguished not only from the media but also from the dominant mode of direct verbal communication that had previously characterized the transmission of jokes." As a result, he continues, the Internet transformed the adversarial, mutually exclusive relationship that existed between the official reactions of mourning in the media and the carnivalesque humor of the catastrophe jokes. In its capacity as a new medium, the Internet gave expression to the elevated discourse of mourning when it transmitted news about the catastrophe, but at the same time, it also assumed the role of direct verbal communications when it provided space for the humorous commentary of jokes. In this way it unified previously fragmented aspects of public morality, which had been separated into a formal-public discourse and an informal-private discourse. (2003, 187)

By 2001 the Internet medium had sufficiently developed to the point where many expressive materials could be faithfully replicated and transcribed online without sacrificing authorial involvement in the process of creation and dissemination—or corrupting the integrity of the intentions behind their expressions. Consequently, many people took to the Internet to reflect and commentate about the attacks with others, which yielded a voluminous display of vernacular expression. As folklorist Rosemary V. Hathaway notes, "9/11 'disaster lore' differed from previous cycles most significantly in its pictorial emphasis" (2005, 44). Photoshopped images of the World Trade Center, narrative accounts of survivors and witnesses, or the sharing of numerous jokes aimed at terrorists or the events themselves circulated ubiquitously.

Like other mass-mediated disasters such as the Challenger space shuttle explosion, people sought reprieve from the hegemonic gatekeepers of information in the media through interaction within the folk-moderated dwellings of cyberspace. After 9/11, Americans took care to symbolically show their unity with those directly affected by the tragedy, either through donations of time, money, or self, displaying visual or textual symbols of solidarity such as supportive bumper stickers or signs, an article of clothing, a flag, or something along those lines (see Kuipers 2005, 77–79). Online, numerous images of the Twin Towers were manipulated to rhetorically assert the resilience of the United States, such as the unapologetic rendering of a "New Design for Rebuilding the World Trade Center," which consisted of five towers lined up in a way that looked like a hand defiantly "flipping the bird," presumably at al-Qaeda. Similarly, images appeared of the Statue of Liberty also rhetorically giving the middle finger, or alternatively holding up Osama bin Laden's severed head in place of her torch.

Indeed, aggression was a predominant theme in a good portion of the Photoshopped humor of 9/11. However, as sociologist Giselinde Kuipers notes, the "hostility in these [aggressive-style] jokes was usually aimed at bin Laden, sometimes at Afghanistan or the Taliban, and some cases, at the American government. Only very rarely was the aggression aimed at Muslims in general. . . . The aggression and degradation were mostly expressed visually, rather than in words" (2011, 32). Osama bin Laden was the most common antagonist, and he was portrayed as being anally penetrated by a camel or being dismembered, tortured, maimed, or humiliated in some way (including through the disparagement of his religious beliefs and appearance). Highly sexual and aggressive material was frequently incorporated. Clearly, such images were not suitable for publication in mainstream newspapers—which contributed to their appeal—but they nevertheless captured and echoed the angry, hurt, confused, and even vengeful voice of the folk.

The wave of humorous Photoshops of Osama bin Laden followed three major themes: scatological (images featuring defecation, use of bin Laden as toilet paper, feces-related wordplay), ethnic (incorporating and/or mocking Middle Eastern customs, using images of magic carpets and camels), and sexual (with bin Laden anally penetrated, feminized, or emasculated); all had vengeful overtones and hinted of (or explicitly promised) imminent, satisfying retaliation (Frank 2004, 642–46; see also Ellis 2003; Kuipers 2011, 28–29, 33–35). However, it is important to note that the technique underlying these jokes was "genre play," which utilized "visual symbolism well known from other genres" (Kuipers 2011, 37). Drawing on popular imagery, especially items that are highly recognizable in many individuals' cultural inventories, humorous uses of the film *Star Wars*, casting bin Laden as a Darth Vader figure in one image (see fig. 6), or the invocation of King Kong, with the caption "Where was King Kong when we needed him?"—drawing on the mammoth creature's famous climb up the Empire State building and swatting away planes in the classic film—helped to reduce the tragedy into a relatively safe and understandable frame. But why?

European philosopher Slavoj Žižek contends that "September 11 can only be understood within the framework of simulation, as Hollywood films and various dramas in U.S. television have already explained to us what events like this are, what they mean, and so on" (Gournelos and Greene 2011, xxvii). Giselinde Kuipers further expands on this sentiment, commenting that

> many people watching television on September 11 remarked how "unreal" it all seemed—yet so familiar: images of wars and exploding skyscrapers are part and parcel of popular culture. Internet jokes referring to action movies such as *Die Hard* (set in a New York skyscraper assaulted by terrorists) explicitly articulate the similarity between images from popular culture and these events.

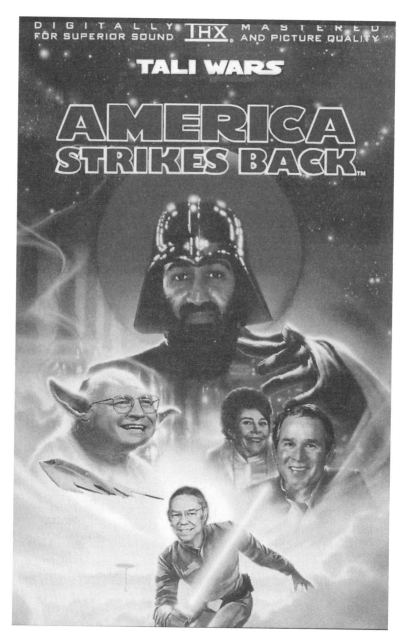

Figure 6. Drawing on the mass appeal of the classic *Star Wars* film *The Empire Strikes Back* (1980), "Tali Wars: America Strikes Back" serves as a symbolic cultural analogy, charged with the task of recasting the present catastrophe into a fictional, manageable frame. Osama bin Laden plays the villainous Darth Vader character, while President George W. Bush is Han Solo (flanked by First Lady, Laura, who doubles as Princess Leia); Vice President Dick Cheney is the fittingly 900-year-old Yoda, and Secretary of State Colin Powell assumes the role of Luke Skywalker.

Media users have been "trained" to respond to messages and images in a specific way. Grief and tears are usually restricted to the genre of drama, explosions to the action movie, burning skyscrapers to the disaster movie. When disaster strikes, what are supposed to be "fictional" events enter into "the news." (2011, 40–41)

As a result, many individuals—at least initially—related to the 9/11 attacks by drawing on cultural analogies that symbolically captured the gravity of what had occurred. So rather than seriously contemplate the loss of nearly 3,000 lives, or the ways that 9/11 "changed everything," it was much easier to recall action movie star Arnold Schwarzenegger (or any popular actor) mowing down terrorists with laughable ease through the frame of one of his films. Rosemary V. Hathaway seems to agree, noting that a "hallmark of 9/11 narratives is an inability to process the events as part of everyday life; only through a cinematic filter can they be understood as 'real'" (2005, 43).

Functionally, then, "Internet jokes can be interpreted as a joking attempt to put these disasters back to where they usually are, where we feel they belong, and where we want them to stay: into the fictional, pleasurable domain of (American) popular culture" (Kuipers 2011, 41; see also Kuipers 2005, 76–80; Malmsheimer 1986). The cultural inventory was once again employed to provide a psychological "night light" and keep weary minds in a state of suspended disbelief, coaxed into processing serious matters in unserious ways. These anxiety-reducing and/or playful tactics represent a salient pattern in how Americans culturally respond in the wake of disaster or shocking news. As the Internet and other new media technology has continued to develop, the need for documenting and analyzing these emergent cultural productions has only become greater.

These popularly circulating, post-9/11 Photoshops were fashioned as a kind of digital collage, and the creative techniques were (and continue to be) "used deliberately and self-consciously, . . . ensuring the process of 'cut and paste' underlying the joke remains evident" (Kuipers 2002, 462, quoted in Hathaway 2005, 45). In other words, viewers of such humor are fully aware that the Photoshopped images are fake, and thus able to decode the incongruity infused within the image.[12] Of course, this was not always the case.

Like the text-oriented e-mail hoaxes and chain letters from years past, another impetus for the creation of Photoshop art derived from artists' desire to produce a realistic "fake" image—either to deceive others as a practical joke or for their own amusement, or as an artistic challenge imbued with its own virtues as a creative endeavor. Perhaps the most notorious instance of this kind of Photoshopped art was the "Tourist Guy" picture hoax (see fig. 7). The seemingly amazing and chilling image appears to capture an unknown white male standing atop the World Trade Center as an incoming plane—the hijacked plane—approaches directly behind him. The date of "09 11 01" is etched into the bottom right-hand corner of the image to indicate "proof" of a timestamp. The image's authenticity is further crystallized by the widely circulated story that the photograph was developed from a camera found among the rubble at Ground Zero.

While initially confounding many of the individuals who saw it, the image quickly came under scrutiny and was soon debunked after several anomalies in the photo were identified: the incoming plane was not appearing blurry, despite its high speeds; neither the man (nor the photographer) appeared to be aware that a loud, incoming plane was right behind them; the man's clothing was rather heavy for a day when the temperature was in the upper sixties and low seventies; and the 110-story plummet seemed too great a distance to reasonably believe that a mere disposable camera could withstand the fall. Within a couple months, a Hungarian man by the name of Peter Guzli reluctantly

Figure 7. This image of the ever-elusive "Tourist Guy" became one of the most widely circulated and hotly contested Photoshop "hoaxes" of all time and also set a folkloric precedent to be emulated in subsequent intricate, eerily convincing Photoshop hoaxes.

admitted to being "Tourist Guy," claiming that he made the image as a prank on some friends, but that it was sent out and quickly spiraled out of control. Once the image was debunked (which symbolically removed the pseudo-realm of respect), numerous users proceeded to make new "Tourist Guy" Photoshops of their own—ranging from manipulations of the "original" image to include additional people or background distractions to cropping "Tourist Guy" himself and placing him in numerous exotic locales from around the world, including scenes from popular movies and even historical moments (see Foster 2012; Frank 2011, 76–82). "Tourist Guy" became a symbolic embodiment of 9/11 for many—and it was a symbol that was malleable through the act of creation. Using the original Tourist Guy image as a template, the wealth of Photoshopped art that followed demonstrated the unmistakable presence of repetition and variation at work.

Like many urban legends, the believability of the Tourist Guy story really took hold because of the e-mail narrative that typically accompanied the mass-forwarded image's dissemination: "This picture was developed from film in a camera found in the rebble [*sic*] of the wtc!!!!!! person in picture still not identified" (Frank 2004, 648; see also Hathaway 2005, 42–45). While this narrative helped to sell the initial believability of "Tourist Guy," the revelation that it was a hoax sprouted "updated" Tourist Guy images via e-mail, featuring "newly discovered" pictures of Tourist Guy appearing in numerous moments of twentieth-century world history, such as the John F. Kennedy assassination and the Hindenburg disaster, or showing up at major world tourist attractions such as the Taj Mahal and the Eiffel Tower. Other new, goofy manipulations of the "original" Tourist Guy image also surfaced and included characters from popular culture in the image's background.

Folklorist Rosemary V. Hathaway (2005) astutely likens the Tourist Guy to "the legendary traveling garden gnome, with added humor in the fact that—like many exhausted travelers—Tourist Guy wears the same indifferent expression regardless of his surroundings" (43). But perhaps most appropriately, Russell Frank (2004) concludes that "Tourist Guy is the quintessence of being in the wrong place at the wrong time. In his ignorance of what is about to befall him, he represents all of us on the morning of September 11" (651).

Beyond the popularity of the images themselves, what causes something to continue disseminating? Is it based on more than just the humor? Writing about the dissemination of e-mailed chain letters, communications scholar Marjorie Kibby notes that the arbitrary sending and receiving of narrative texts seems "to give the e-mailer an even greater sense of distance from the content, . . . [and] [w]hile this detachment lessens accountability, at the same time it increases authenticity" (2005, 772). In other words, when a joke or narrative is e-mailed to an individual imploring them to forward it on to others, the authoritative and anonymous nature of the text's origins diminishes one's sense of ownership or accountability over the content as he or she sends it. This makes the material appear more authentic and worthy of subsequent transmission. In doing so, users reflexively circulate materials that may be subversive and/or bring them pleasure without having to directly acknowledge as much. In sending the material along, one is simply a conduit in the rapid dissemination of folklore. Photoshops, when created as a hoax, operate similarly but on a visual level. After all, as the proverb goes, seeing *is* believing. Still, in both cases, the remaining "X" factor is that purveyors of folklore can just as easily jump in and create, modify, communicate, and/or participate in the process as they can remain in a passive role. As greater computer literacy continues to take hold, this fact will be of even greater importance and interest to contemporary folklorists.

Giselinde Kuipers contends that "disaster jokes about the events of September 11 are a comment on the moral and emotional language of the American media culture as a whole—of which both the discourse on disaster and the humor discourse are a part" (2011, 43). This is especially important to note with regard to 9/11 humor that surfaced long after the initial waves of humor reverberated through cyberspace (see Ellis 2001, 2003). In the weeks, months, and years following the attacks, the United States ignited a global "War on Terror," which led to major military conflicts in Afghanistan and Iraq, as well as the creation of numerous domestic initiatives aimed at ensuring greater national security. These government-led programs became notoriously mocked for their overwhelmingly patriotic and alarmist rhetoric, as evidenced on the government website Ready.gov (which dispensed vague advice on how to prepare for a terrorist attack [see "Duct and Cover" 2003]), or for how these new programs impinged on existing civil liberties (with airport security protocols a frequent target).[13]

The highly visual response to 9/11 also bled into subsequent disaster responses such as those seen in the aftermath of Hurricane Katrina, most famously in a widely circulating Photoshopped image that shows President George W. Bush and his father fishing in the flooded streets of New Orleans. The Photoshop rhetorically critiques (and echoes the public perception of) the Bush administration's inappropriately lackadaisical response to the catastrophe. This image and many others were easily accessible on the Internet (see Frank 2009, 2011), and these artistic expressions helped to inform and establish the folkloric precedent for responding to subsequent large-scale disasters, such as

Figure 8. In this illustration of the death of Aquaman, digital folk art takes aim at British Petroleum. The illustration was originally created by Nick Cardy and subsequently Photoshopped by New Jersey artist Rob Kelly, who hosts the blog *The Aquaman Shrine* (www.aquamanshrine.com). In this fictional comic book cover, legendary superhero (and all-around underwater action enthusiast) Aquaman succumbs to the effects of the massive BP oil spill in the Gulf of Mexico that began in April 2010 and went unsuccessfully treated for months afterward. Shortly after this image was posted on Kelly's blog on May 22, 2010 (http://www.aquaman shrine .com/2010/05/sg.html), it quickly went viral and was widely distributed via e-mail and numerous other news and pop-culture-oriented websites. Furthermore, it was overwhelmingly applauded for its timely and cleverly packaged critique of the concurrent fallout from the oil spill.

the BP oil spill–inspired digital folk art, which display expressive motifs that may be classified as traditional (see fig. 8). The art created in response to the BP oil spill, in particular, relied heavily on images and figures from popular culture to be effective.

With the death of 9/11 mastermind Osama bin Laden on May 2, 2011, following a raid at his secret Pakistani compound, the visual humorous forms that emerged nearly a decade earlier came full circle. In many ways, the visual dimension of humor was brought to the fore, but with the incorporation of text to juxtapose humorous rhetoric with manipulated images. The largely celebratory feeling surrounding the death of bin Laden led to much lighter Photoshopped humor in comparison with the occasionally aggressive and vengeful tone during 9/11—and the distinction is rather self-explanatory, given the emotional impact of the respective events. Since taking office, President Barack Obama had been routinely criticized by conservative politicians, pundits, and members of the "birther" movement who believed that the president was not a real U.S. citizen and demanded to see his birth certificate. Not even a week before the bin Laden raid, though, the president finally *did* release his complete birth certificate to silence his critics. Thus, one of the first images to surface after the bin Laden raid (and numerous similar images appeared with slightly amended text and different photographs—all of which show an exultant shot of the president) poked fun at the people who had spent so much wasted energy on trying to undermine his credibility. One popularly circulating Photoshop featured President Obama heading onto Air Force One, smiling, wearing sunglasses, and pointing toward the camera lens with a hint of swagger. The accompanying words scroll across the image in two lines: "Sorry it took so long to get you a copy of my birth certificate. I was too busy killing Osama bin Laden."

Social networking services played a prominent role in spreading the news of bin Laden's demise, whereas they were not yet available when 9/11 took place. Facebook and especially Twitter led to the incredibly fast dissemination of the news about bin Laden's death once it was confirmed. Within hours of the news making headlines, numerous people in cities and towns all across America spontaneously gathered in the streets to celebrate the righteous execution of the mastermind behind the terrorist attacks of September 11, 2011. In State College, Pennsylvania, where I was living at the time, the downtown morphed into a sea of red, white, and blue until the wee hours of the morning, with folks singing patriotic songs in unison (in addition to getting drunk).

But perhaps the pervasiveness of social media was most evident *during* the very raid in which Osama bin Laden was killed. Two Pakistani men living in the vicinity of bin Laden's compound took to Twitter to remark and complain about the unusual sounds and activity that seemed to be taking place in a relatively close proximity (Couts 2011). In doing so, however, they managed to inadvertently chronicle the entire raid—and all in 144-character increments at a time, no less![14] Facebook and Twitter were often characters in bin Laden death humor, often in the form of fake Facebook posts and exchanges between bin Laden and other parties. For example, one circulating Photoshop depicted Osama bin Laden updating his Facebook status to "BRB Someone's at the door. I think it's the pizza guy," which is then "liked" by the U.S. Navy SEALs, the implication of course being that they (the SEALs) are the "pizza guy" and ol' Osama is in for a big, deathly surprise.

Several fake Twitter accounts were operated by individuals who humorously pretended to be Osama bin Laden, both before and after the raid—before the raid, they would tweet updates with exaggerated remarks and silly activities;

Figure 9. In this candid photograph of the Obama "situation room" taken by White House photographer Pete Souza, the Obama administration and other key personnel watch a live feed of the raid on Osama bin Laden's Pakistani complex. The image was posted to the White House's open access Flickr account and quickly set new records in garnering nearly two million views in less than two days (http://www.flickr.com/photos/whitehouse/5680724572/). It has since been described by scholars and media pundits as a "historic" image that may capture the "defining moment in Barack Obama's presidency."

Figure 10. The Obama situation room . . . literally. This is an early example of repetition and variation stemming from the widespread dissemination of the release of the original situation room photograph.

Figure 11. In a flurry of cut-and-paste tomfoolery, this Photoshop of the original situation room photo shows a more extreme example of repetition and variation at work. Not only are previous "Tourist Guy" conventions thematically included (namely the wacky incorporation of pop culture figures whenever possible) but the seriousness of the image itself is also lampooned.

after bin Laden was killed they would provide cheeky tweets with content such as "It's really hot down here."[15] But mocking impersonators were not the only ones to get in on the act; other regular individuals also offered up some crude topical humor. One person tweeted, "I'd be scared if I was Michelle Obama's pussy right now." And suggesting the continuing impact of the traditions imposed by the "Tourist Guy" phenomenon of 9/11 was the widespread Photoshopping of the Obama "Situation Room" picture (see fig. 9). The original image captured key members of the Obama administration as they were watching the dramatic, real-time video feed of the bin Laden raid as it progressed. Unlike the "Tourist Guy" image, this photograph *was* real; however, both images similarly portrayed scenarios in which the actors are calm and resolute, despite the tense context that surrounds the scene. And since both images featured individuals who were not harmed, they became fodder for Photoshop play. The "Situation Room" had dozens of variations, but most of them again drew on references to popular culture to be most effective (see figs. 10 and 11).

In the context of a mass-mediated disaster, Photoshopped humor promotes the manipulation of "real" images in order to offset the psychological distress or anxiety associated with an ongoing calamity—or in some cases even celebrate a death (as was the case with Osama bin Laden). Users can symbolically re-situate or (if desired) undermine the event's entire meaning by creatively producing an image that humorously addresses it. Photoshops may also serve as a means for the folk to rhetorically supplement or contest news coverage; after all, as they are vernacular, they are not bound by the same rules or social conventions as professional journalists are.

Following a calamitous event, such as a mass shooting or terrorist attack, one (or many individuals) may feel incensed to the point where their feelings cannot be adequately represented or conveyed through conventional channels. Photoshopped humor not only diminishes the emotional impact of a tragedy and/or how it is being portrayed in the media, but it also imposes a revised narrative that gives creators and consumers a semblance of control over an otherwise uncertain or upsetting time. As a digital creation, it is incredibly easy to transmit; popular images are able to disseminate very rapidly. Many Photoshopped images also incorporate figures and elements from popular culture into the art, thereby tapping into a collective body of material that is widely archived in the cultural inventories of those who are most likely to view the image (see Frank 2004, 2011; Kuipers 2002, 2005).[16] As sociologist Giselinde Kuipers argues, "Visual jokes defy the moral discourse of the media, provide the pleasure of boundary transgression, and block feelings of involvement. . . . These jokes do not build community or stress solidarity, but set the jokers apart from public discourse, and presumably, mainstream sentiments" (2005, 81).

At first glance, venturing into the online world to relieve stress in times of anxiety or make social connections with strangers may appear to be an escape from reality. However, this virtual "escape" is simply an alternative (albeit structurally different) simulated reality—one that is more pliable and capable of meeting individual needs with instant gratification. Surely, this circumvention of restrictive social environments is enticing in times of communal anxiety. This freedom affords individuals the ability to protest or mock hegemonic forces in their lives such as the corporate office, educational institutions, the mass media, or their government. Understanding *how* and *why* people use technology to process their feelings or diffuse anxiety is of paramount importance.

Because laughter is a predominantly social, not biological, phenomenon (Provine 2000), the interactivity of the Internet medium is of tremendous value in processing ideas about tumultuous events or people. The following chapter contemplates these factors through an examination of the folk sentiments regarding the media's coverage of celebrities and their personal lives.

CHAPTER 4

჈

"Intimate Strangers"

THE FOLK RESPONSE TO
CELEBRITY DEATH AND FALLS FROM GRACE

Until this point, I have discussed at great length the mass-mediated disasters, the human need for connectivity, and the historical contexts through
which vernacular expression has been facilitated by mass media in the response
to tragedy. So how, then, does celebrity and folk culture meaningfully inter-
sect within society, and why does it matter? Surprisingly, celebrity culture
provides compelling evidence for how new media technologies influence folkloric dissemination after a death, tragedy, or scandal breaks. Juicy stories on
superstars' scandals or reportage on domestic natural disasters have attracted
folklore in the form of rumors, cautionary tales, or jokes in years past, but the
mainstream acceptance of the Internet as a communications tool complicates
previous notions about the nature of narrative transmission.

This chapter examines the American infatuation with celebrities and the
observable consequences that celebrities face when a preconceived notion of
their persona disintegrates. In particular, I explore the folk conceptualization
of celebrities and how the mass media facilitates both the construction and
deconstruction of these suppositions. By examining the folk response to
media coverage of celebrities in tabloids and on the Internet, I argue that communal ideals are in part socially constructed through symbolic interaction.
Celebrity culture provides a salient window into the folk process in times of
anxiety, as a star's fall from grace or involvement in a scandal is often presented
similarly to large-scale tragedies and disasters in the mass media, thus evoking
similar responses.

Many joke tellers and their audiences reaffirm societal expectations of behavior and fidelity by using celebrities as symbols for overarching values and
causes that they wish to emulate. When a celebrity symbolically engenders
particular values or standards, most violations of the aims that they represent

will result in rhetorical denigration within individual cultural inventories and imaginary social worlds. Doing so protects the balance, morality, and integrity of the individual's worldview. While celebrity *faux pas* may not be equitable to the terrorist attacks of 9/11 or the chaotic aftermath of Hurricane Katrina, the subsequent process of vernacular expression is nearly identical in the digital age. Just as the response to large-scale disasters reveals cultural anxieties, prejudices, rumors, beliefs, and a pendulum of opinions as individuals make sense of the chaos and reassure themselves (see Fine 1992), the folk response to celebrities reveals a similar social function as a mediator and conduit of imaginary social relationships.

The word "celebrity" is derived from the Latin word *celebritas*, meaning "fame" or "renown." Historian Daniel Boorstin famously defined our modern understanding of a celebrity succinctly as "*a person who is known for his well-knownness*" (1961, 57, emphasis in original). However, historically speaking, the modern conceptualization of celebrity has evolved from the archaic conceptualization of "renown," or the esteemed reputation of monarchs and the virility of statesmen, created largely from the spectacle of their public appearances and decrees (Inglis 2010; see also Fine 2001). Indeed, early conceptualizations of what we would now call "celebrity" were attached to the most accomplished or politically powerful individuals—more important, to those with an active and visible role within their community or nation. This model of renown crossed the Atlantic Ocean from Europe to colonial America, and the earliest American "real-life" folk heroes (such as George Washington, Benjamin Franklin, and Betsy Ross) have engendered an authoritative recollection in history as symbols of model stature, ability, and notoriety for their personal feats. Undoubtedly, some of their feats were embellished and circulated through folklore during their lives, and these feats surely underwent revision and reinterpretation over the years.[1] Be that as it may, the narrative of these individuals' importance to early America's symbolic identity has made them revered figures even in the present.

The emergence of Hollywood's "star system," which lasted until the 1940s, witnessed the practice of film studios creating new names and identities for attractive actors in an effort to glamorize their public personas and emphasize their image over talent; this helped to shift perceptions of celebrity into more aesthetic territory (see McDonald 2001). Public figures had to balance their ideological stances and personal quirks with the ability to connect with their audiences, while also developing a public persona and general "image" to maintain—the emphasis on the visual marked a stark change in the symbolic values assigned to such famous individuals. These individuals were received in aesthetic and symbolic terms and were judged by their ability to performatively conform to the socially constructed values and expectations of those who admired them.

By the 1960s and 1970s, many households owned a television set and the nightly news consequently invaded the living rooms of everyday people for the first time ever on a large scale. Thanks to the widespread adoption of the home television set, the shock of President Kennedy's assassination, the horrors of the Vietnam War, and the disappointment of the Watergate scandal were palpable images, narratives, and memories for the average American. Within the context of an unsettled world, American society was rocked by the angst and social upheaval of a changing culture. Visual reportage covered everything going right, and especially what was going *wrong*. At the movie theater or at home with their television sets, people became emotionally connected to the individuals who appeared before them. The celebrities who emerged during this era not only provided a reprieve from the very real, grim images that were invading viewers' cultural inventories but also acted as fantastical symbols that provided quiet comfort in uncertain times.

Today, the threshold for celebrity status has evolved to recognize individuals who do not acquire fame or renown through their symbolic leadership or cultural benefit to mass society but rather through their recognizable presence in popular culture. As a result, select individuals who have talent in an area of public interest—sports, film and television, or music, for example—are now able to achieve a revered status previously reserved for heads of state, revolutionaries, and social pioneers. More important, the transformation into a "celebrity" can take place in a relatively short amount of time. The never-ending rush of consumerism in American culture allows for performers and athletes to be quickly swept up into the fray of popular culture; they become commodities that are packaged, sold, and consumed.[2] But more than that, these individuals become our "intimate strangers"—those whom we know, but in reality do *not* know.

Imaginary Social Worlds and Celebrity Culture Consumption

Owing to the onslaught of gossip columns, magazines, tabloids, television programs (both satirical and genuine), web-based news dissemination, and now, even more ubiquitously, amateur and professional blogging, every detail of celebrity culture is filtered, scrutinized, and presented through a vast web of opinion, manipulation, and perpetual exchange. Celebrities are treated as if they are our neighbors, ordinary folks whom we know personally or intimately, as well as professionally.[3] From gossip magazines to TMZ.com, narratives of celebrities "gone wild" abound in numerous forms of popular media, often glamorizing their seemingly deliberate social deviance. Some entertainment magazines publish pictures of celebrities without makeup or display shots of them doing "normal" things to prove that they really are "just like us," while others look to get "dirt" on celebrities. Such exposure embeds within the public an inordinate amount of knowledge about many celebrities' film and television projects as well as personal information about their individual hobbies, humanitarian causes in which they participate, their sex lives, or even their proclivity for adopting children from third-world countries. Celebrities are aware of such headline-grabbing motifs, too, and seem to frequently invoke the pop culture proverb, "there's no such thing as bad publicity," in having their publicists—media specialists by trade—manipulate paparazzi and fans to follow their supposedly glamorous lives. Our cultural inventories are flooded with data. As anthropologist John L. Caughey (1984) observes, "Media figures play significant roles in both memories and anticipations. In memories, the individual often replays segments from past media productions he or she has witnessed. Fans often do this deliberately, and typically they can recall their favorite scenes in the most vivid detail. Most informants also regularly experience spontaneous stream-of-consciousness replays of past media scenes. Often an environmental perception will suggest a media image and lead the individual's consciousness inward into a recall of social scenes from a book, newspaper, or movie" (136). Recall for a moment the constellation of celebrities or famous individuals whose résumés, personalities, or public personas are easily retrieved from your own cultural inventory. Think of actors, athletes, musicians, authors, columnists, television personalities (from news anchors and talk show hosts to infomercial pitchmen and evangelists), businessmen, entrepreneurs, inventors, and politicians whom you can recollect. In conjunction with the cultural inventory, these individuals make up our artificial or *"imaginary" social worlds*—the interpersonal links that we make with public figures, celebrities, and other people whom we do not know in our personal lives but nevertheless interact with frequently owing to a rapport developed through mass-mediated outlets.

    The number of individuals who make up our imaginary social worlds often include several times as many persons as those in our "real" social worlds, which are composed of friends, family, and acquaintances (Caughey 1984, 32). As odd as it may seem, "imaginary" relationships actually serve an important function as a means of conceptualizing, as well as cognitively prioritizing and organizing, the desirable qualities that we hope to emulate and invite into our social lives. While we do not actually know the famous individuals who litter our cultural inventories and social worlds in the same way that we know a spouse or a close friend, we paradoxically *do* know them. Rhetorically (just as a real friend might), they make us laugh, they report on our constituents, or they find common ground and validate our worldviews in a public forum through their actions or publicized ideologies. They are real, living people with real experiences, and in a peculiar way, they do appear to be a part of our lives. As Richard Schickel notes: "Most of us retain, in most of our private and professional dealings with people we don't actually know, a sense of their otherness, a decent wariness that protects both ourselves and the stranger from intrusion. But that shyness . . . is not operative when we are dealing with celebrities. Thanks to television and the rest of the media we *know* them, or think we do. To a greater or lesser degree, we have internalized them, unconsciously made them a part of our consciousness, just as if they were, in fact, friends" (Schickel 1985, 4). In other words, while we may intentionally avoid a full-fledged relationship with a co-worker who has peripheral, matching interests (but lacks the promise of mutual compatibility necessary for a sustained friendship), we actively nurture a psychological connection to celebrities in a very real and personal way—even though they are not active or physically present in our lives.[4] In the pursuit of meaningful connections with other humans, celebrity culture provides an alternate avenue for achieving intimacy. More to the point, in the absence of physical connectivity, imaginary social relationships help to compensate for the lack of meaningful, symbolic contact in the analog, or physical, world.[5]

An exemplary case of the folk response to a celebrity who maintained an imaginary social relationship with many people can be observed in the passing of Gary Coleman on May 28, 2010. Like the folklore that appeared after the Challenger disaster, the Internet provided the means for people to process the loss of a person with whom they had an imaginary social relationship—often with rhetoric that incorporated knowledge from their cultural inventories (about his career, the context of his death, or his physical attributes or limitations). Some representative examples in online circulation shortly following news of his passing:

Today, flags will not be flown at half-staff, but at 4 feet 8 inches off the ground.

I'm observing a half-moment of silence for Gary Coleman.

. . . Such a short lived life.

Before he died, Actor Gary Coleman was released from a Utah jail after being arrested on a warrant for failing to appear in court. The court regrets the error and promises to give Coleman a milk crate to stand on next time.

A week before his death, Utah police say actor Gary Coleman hit a man with his pickup after an argument at a bowling alley; . . . after getting out of his truck, Coleman continued beating the man with one of the dozen Los Angeles phone books he was sitting on to see over the dashboard.

Gary Coleman's passing proves once again that it's better to be dead than in Utah.

Gary Coleman, former child star, has died at the age of 42. Doctors blame his death on complications from "different strokes" [the name of the television show in which Coleman starred earlier in his career].

Gary Coleman? I sure did like his coolers, tents, lanterns and camp stoves. He will be missed.

As these examples indicate, Gary Coleman's death attracted rather mean-spirited humor that made fun of his size, acting resume, and erratic personal life.

This was also the case following the death of singer Amy Winehouse on July 23, 2011, which also occurred on the same day that a Norwegian gunman murdered over ninety people, many of whom were children, and planted bombs in Oslo. The very serious and unfolding tragedy in Norway stood in stark contrast to Winehouse's alcohol-induced death; consequently, the direction of humor became predictable and also took attention away from the gruesomeness of the "other" big story (in fact, I observed numerous cases where joke tellers openly stated this to be the case).

To be sure, Amy Winehouse was lauded for her unmistakable musical talents by critics and peers, but she also endured crippling and very public battles with drug and alcohol addiction, which dampened others' threshold for sympathy. As a result, she was unabashedly lampooned within moments of her death being announced. Within a period of four hours, the sick joke wiki site, Sickipedia, hosted over thirty-two pages of user-submitted jokes and mean-spirited comments. On Twitter and Facebook, the news quickly spread and invited a folk response; numerous individuals—regular folks and celebrities alike—posted thoughtful memories and serious messages, while others leapt at the chance to offer up some death humor before the singer's corpse had gone cold. Among the most popular jokes that appeared both immediately and in subsequent weeks, the following examples (which came in numerous variations, but are nevertheless representative) surfaced all over the Internet:

Amy Winehouse died from severe head trauma . . . also known as "Crack Head." (Collected July 23, 2011)

Congratulations to Amy Winehouse on 24 hours of sobriety. (Collected July 24, 2011)

Amy Winehouse took more shots in her arm than a Norwegian youth camp. (Collected July 24, 2011)

Q: What was Amy Winehouse's biggest hit?
A: Her last one! (Collected July 25, 2011)

Q: What's the difference between Amy Winehouse and a Moped?
A: A Moped can hit 30. [Winehouse died at age 27] (Collected July 25, 2011)

It seems like this is the end of the line for Amy Winehouse. (Collected July 27, 2011)

Elton John will be performing at Amy Winehouse's funeral with a beautiful rendition of "Candle Under the Spoon." (Collected July 28, 2011)

Other jokes played off the lyrics and meter of Winehouse's most successful single, "Rehab." Beginning with the song's actual opening lyrics, "They tried to make me go to rehab," the jokes then replaced the original subsequent lyrics ("but I said no, no, no") with humorous wordplay variations: "but I should've said yes, yes, yes"; "but now I'm dead, dead, dead"; "but now I'm gone, gone, gone"; and "but I said, *THUD*," among other renditions.

Numerous other jokes also invoked materials from popular culture and their individual cultural inventories, alluding to the film *Pulp Fiction* (1994) and to the then-current spectacle of actor Charlie Sheen's peculiar behavior and rantings during several 2011 television interviews. Most interestingly, in chronicling several different websites for six straight hours from the moment I heard of Amy Winehouse's death (approximately two hours after it had been announced), it was clear that the materials being posted to the site were far more refined and compositionally "tight" than the initial offerings—an indicator of the rapid dissemination of humor and proof of folklore's repetition and variation in an online context.

In any case, in the socially ascribed hierarchy of celebrities and their perceived value to popular culture and the imaginary social worlds of their admirers, Gary Coleman and Amy Winehouse were not as particularly valued as contemporaries like Michael Jackson or Farrah Fawcett—hence the significant rhetorical differences between the joke repertoires that circulated after their respective deaths.[6] My use of the word "imaginary" is not meant to denote a value judgment on the appropriateness of such relationships. Moreover, I do not mean to use "imaginary" or "simulative" to suggest that there is a lack of meaning in place. In fact, many of these artificial relationships are quite real and meaningful to the individuals. When describing such pseudoconnections to celebrities, I use terms such as imagined, illusion, or fantasy social worlds and relationships interchangeably throughout to signify associations that are not forged from casual interaction among peers in the analog world; however, I am generally referring to the same thing. I should clarify that the fantasy of imaginary social relationships is often a considerably personal process, "both because it is a private experience that takes place within the individual's mind, and because it is the product of the individual's psychological needs" (Caughey 1984, 163). Celebrities and media figures are often the object of such relationships because they are easy to enter and the rules of maintenance (or abandonment) are elastic and individualized.

This talk of "imaginary social relationships" or intricate, one-sided fantasies that involve celebrities may sound pathological, but it is not (Caughey 1984; see also Dixon 1999; Inglis 2010; Marshall 2006; Schickel 1985). For example, imagine a person who loyally tunes into the local news to catch the five-day forecast every night at 6:00 p.m. This display of loyalty to a single meteorologist exemplifies an inherently artificial relationship. Perhaps because the person has proven to be an accurate forecaster (or because he or she has a pleasant delivery), the viewer at home develops a rapport with this individual, noting that this person is someone who can be trusted or counted on as they go about making plans. The meteorologist is aware of a general viewership, but does not reciprocate the intimate relationship with the individual viewer. Nevertheless, the viewer at home continues to frequent the local news station at 6:00 p.m. to see what this reliable acquaintance has to say. It is not crazy to model such behavior, and indeed many people follow the same routine with their own trusty meteorologists.

To be sure, a rapport with "intimate strangers" is present in many rhetorical interactions with celebrities and public figures found in the media's crosshairs. Such a rapport can be observed when individuals dress as a character, attempt to embody a celebrity's essence, or wear a favorite athlete's jersey.[7] So, too, when an amateur garage band covers a popular song, when video game enthusiasts channel rock stardom in Guitar Hero, when someone imitates or quotes dialogue from a favorite movie or television program, or when someone sexually fantasizes about an attractive celebrity. These are not examples of pathological behavior but rather examples of a mind at play—or in a state of suspended reality that gives pleasure—and serves to ease the sterility or complexities of day-to-day life. This kind of fantasy is a cultural phenomenon that "reflects individual desires, but only as these have been shaped, twisted, and structured by social and cultural forces" (Caughey 1984, 163). Thus, imagined social relationships with celebrities and media personalities are not only common and normal but also functional as a means of refining the illusion of connectivity to the outside world. In sum, these pseudorelationships are valuable as a psychological simulation of intimacy in the digital age.

Of course, there are more extreme examples of fantasized relationships with celebrities or media figures that are most certainly pathological (see Caughey 1984, 1–7; Schickel 1985). Mark David Chapman was obsessed with John Lennon's music career and grew angry at interview comments that he made, as well as the nuances of his music, and ultimately killed him in December 1980. John Hinckley Jr., Ronald Reagan's would-be assassin, was obsessed with Jodie Foster after seeing her portrayal of a teenage prostitute in *Taxi Driver* (1976) and sought meaningful, "real" contact with her, and even stalked her at times. When these tactics failed to garner her attention, he resorted to even more outlandish means of "winning her affection and love," and sent her numerous letters and gifts (Schickel 1985). Beyond these specific examples there are many cases in which individuals have stalked, attacked, or even murdered celebrities (or committed suicide as part of a morbid fantasy). My point here is that while pathological cases of imagined celebrity relationships exist, it is crucial to understand that most people have healthy (albeit dissonant and fantastical) relationships with individuals whom they have never met in person. This is very common in American culture.

At the end of the day many celebrities also serve as a different kind of symbol: extended family. Just as we are quick to let a beloved aunt off the hook for a bad deed or conversely lambast a rival sibling over the slightest trespass, we conceptualize celebrities with similar compartmentalization. The bad ones can never do right; the loved ones, unless unequivocally proven to be otherwise, are often infallible. Like family, celebrities who fall from grace or pass away also require a sense of closure for the individuals who have followed them. Redemption—whether through the celebrity's apologetic actions and rhetoric or a posthumous revision of their memory by mourners—is often sought as a key component of their narrative transformation when their symbolic persona evolves. Celebrity "comeback" stories always play well in the public eye as they represent growth through humility, renewal, reintegration, and perseverance.

When the ideals of an imaginary relationship are infringed upon, disrupted, or otherwise truncated (either by the object of fantasy's actions or outside influence), the illusion becomes unstable and creates an emotional reverberation that forces the imagining individual to act out. In these cases, the Internet and other new media devices serve as a breeding ground for vernacular expression in response to celebrity culture. Of course, this can also be seen online in the folk response to many other newsworthy happenings—including disaster, tragedy, politically charged debates, or even gossip column "comment" sections—because of the widespread availability and instantaneity of digital technology as a medium for computer-mediated communication.

The digital interactions that stem from a shared interest (or revulsion) about a particular topic, event, or person often yield a different kind of relationship structure than the comparably "imaginary" construct between an individual and an admired celebrity or public figure. Thus, a terminological distinction may serve to distinguish these relationships from those that are forged online between mutually committed parties but nevertheless also lack the corporeality of face-to-face or in-person intimacy.

Simulative Social Worlds and the
Response to Mass Media

The patterns of community building and online vernacular expression that are forged between individuals in shared online space represent the cultivation of *simulative social worlds*. In contrast to imaginary social worlds, which are inherently one-sided in that they do not elicit two-way communication between a public figure and the admiring individual, simulative social worlds signify relationships that are created, maintained, and fostered through online interaction between fellow Internet users.[8] The interactions that take place in the online venues where meaningful expression and dialogue occur—blogs, forums, website comment sections, online gaming—allow for a communicative exchange that features a reciprocal communicator-receiver dynamic. Artificial personal connections to celebrities and public figures are peripheral and internally regulated. By contrast, simulative social connections online allow for emotional validation regarding the investment of a fellow user's time, energy, and/or trust by using the computer as a mediatory agent. Even though there is not a physical element to the communal discourse or individual conversations, the emotional connection remains palpable.

Although they are not corporeal, Internet and new media technologies serve a similar psychological function as imaginary social relationships in that they also simulate relationships with other people. Participants converge on the same cyber terrain and are able to interact in real time, often with the intention of expressing themselves either rhetorically or in an effort to contribute to an online community's familial environment. The relationship-building patterns forged through online vernacular expression and symbolic interaction can either be brief and ancillary (as with a harmless "flame war," or in earnest replies to ongoing comments) or, conversely, rather intimate and prolonged, with deep communal connections, traditions, and expectations within the context of a shared online venue.

When the communicative exchange opportunity afforded by computer-mediated communication intersects with the need to comment on the newsworthy actions of celebrities (for better or worse), the biases of the individuals' imaginary social relationships with celebrities come to the fore and merge with the nuances of the simulative social worlds entrenched online. It is here—juxtaposed between the simulative contexts of an online venue and the individual users' own external, imaginary social worlds—where the importance of imaginary social relationships becomes most clear, revealing a great deal about how people construct meaningful connections with others in mass society.

Just as one might defend a friend over an unjust attack, some Internet users will rhetorically announce their loyalty to a beloved celebrity through dismissive dialogue or defensive communication following a controversial news story. Others (perhaps subconsciously testing their peers' like-minded dissatisfaction with a celebrity's deviance) lash out, sometimes humorously or satirically, other times seriously or viciously. In a virtual world where a digital barrier protects users from physical confrontation and harm or social repercussions in their "real" lives, people are able to openly express themselves in a multitude of ways. Given their perception of safety and perceived distance, it stands to reason that many interactions found online may be more genuine than those amongst a group of amicable colleagues reacting to a news story, and thus are more indicative of the true folk response to mass media.

Online, folk values are reestablished through symbolic rhetoric and interaction, and the celebrity under scrutiny is collectively othered as deviant and unworthy of admiration. Groupthink emerges and attempts to reaffirm the online community's moral compass. The lack of an individual's conformity to the group's mood elicits communal scorn. Of course, the failure of individuals to separate themselves from the illusion of intimacy results in a deeper degree of emotional investment in their betrothed celebrity's stature remaining respectable—and denial when this image is destroyed. As Caughey notes, a parasocial relationship with an admired figure—whether through books, television, records, or imagination—is often felt to be subjectively beneficial, but when an admired figure dies, "the person [who admires the celebrity] feels the loss of both friend and mentor" (1984, 66). These emotional responses resemble the loss of a "real" friend, which underscores the true realness of imaginary social relationships for the individual.

Celebrities are expected to embody the best standards of society. They operate in a guarded social bubble where their relationships to "regular" individuals are one-sided and impersonal, yet they are placed on a pedestal where expectation for unwavering, socially acceptable behavior is common. When we encounter people or hear about behaviors or ideas that run counter to our individual notions of right and wrong, good and bad, and so on, we tend to dismiss or reject these people or ideas; in some cases, we even ostracize them in order to create social distance while rhetorically affirming our predetermined values as superior. Some of these dismissals are tacit, while others are public or even performatively undertaken. In these latter cases, a window of opportunity opens for individuals to express their values and cast a metaphorical fishing line into the throws of society, reeling in those who agree with the bait. On the Internet, however, the lack of physicality provides a social buffer for vernacular expression and allows users to do this ideological "fishing" for camaraderie or perhaps even some intentional sparring, just like someone in the analog world may seek out a bar fight.

When living celebrities reveal themselves in a newly negative light, betrayal results, and reconciliation is needed before slanderous or dismissive responses can fade. When celebrities die, admiring individuals are forced to reexamine their feelings about the imaginary relationship with the figure, especially if formal redemption efforts have not taken place, because the relationship is symbolically severed. The cultural loss is a personal one for the individual with emotional ties to the media figure. The emotional responses to celebrities' lives are not limited to instances of death. In fact, any instance in which a once-esteemed media figure comes under fire can elicit emotional responses that would be expected of a betrayal in one's personal circle.

The folk response to celebrity culture reveals the rhetorical markers for societal beliefs and expectations about the individuals whom they often emulate. In doing so, they articulate the folk conceptualization of normalcy and decency. More important, these responses demonstrate a projection of the individual's own subconscious values, helping to cement his or her own ideas as being morally sound. While expressing themselves in a way that elicits feelings of connectivity and intimacy with others via the online venue, individuals are able to compensate for the disruption to their imagined social relationship. Indeed, as Christie Davies notes, "Some sports stars are intelligent, but what matters is that they do not need be. They merely have certain highly specific physical aptitudes that can make them very rich but that have no real use outside that sport" (2011, 39). As a result, this underlying knowledge provides the potential to serve as ammunition for emergent humor on the relative "worthlessness" of a famous individual who was formerly appreciated. For instance, the fact that a "liked" celebrity athlete has twelve children with eight different partners may be no cause for social commentary; however, should they act out in negative ways, or should their level of competitive athleticism diminish, a new door is opened that can tap into this schematic information as a source of humor to contend with the incongruous behavior of siring children out of wedlock, or at least outside a committed relationship.

Like traditional media disasters, celebrities often attract the ire of the public when their level of exposure becomes oversaturated in the media or when their bad behavior crosses the line of social taboos with regard to perversion, fidelity, mental illness, or social deviance. This can be seen in the increasingly negative and dismissive treatment in the media of such celebrities as socialite Paris Hilton, actress Lindsay Lohan, singer Britney Spears, and reality television star Kate Gosselin (of *Jon and Kate Plus 8*). Some celebrity couples have also attracted misgivings from the overexposure of their public affection and were even assigned such abbreviating monikers as "Bennifer" (actor Ben Affleck and singer Jennifer Lopez), "Brangelina" (actors Brad Pitt and Angelina Jolie), and "TomKat" (actors Tom Cruise and Katie Holmes). Beyond overexposure, celebrity deviance has also attracted backlash, as in the case of musician John Mayer's comments on his perception among African Americans (see Cwynar 2010) or the fallout from Michael Richards's use of the "N" word with an audience member during a 2009 comedy show.

A fundamental shift in the focus of celebrity coverage and its subsequent reception transcends simple gawking and prodding into their antics and instead goes deeper psychologically for the telecommunicated media's audience. The audience responds to the seriousness of the celebrity's behavior by projecting their own anxieties about eccentric, criminal, or deviant behaviors into the performance and dissemination of humor. Not only is this data richly evocative of the influence of popular culture on ideas about mental health in society but it also demonstrates how the socially conceived means of information dissemination manifest in contemporary culture. Chapters 5 and 6 of this work are dedicated to two detailed case studies that further illustrate these claims.

CHAPTER 5

❧

From Sports Hero
to Supervillain

OR, HOW TIGER WOODS WRECKED HIS CAR(EER)

There was a time when professional golfer Eldrick "Tiger" Woods could do no wrong. In the minds of many adoring fans and respected sports commentators he was an exemplary professional with sound moral credentials. From his early career through 2009, the charming and handsome athlete was recruited to endorse such high-profile products as Nike shoes and Gatorade sports drinks as well as golf equipment and apparel. He eventually created his own line of clothing and even sponsored a popular video game franchise bearing his name and likeness. In addition to the admirable persona that Woods and his public relations team promoted, the fact remains that he was actually an immensely talented and entertaining athlete who broke numerous professional golfing records before reaching age twenty-five. As a biracial individual of African American and Thai heritage, Woods was also portrayed in the media as a groundbreaking figure in the predominantly white sport of golf and applauded as a positive role model for children and minorities. Above all, Tiger Woods's success as a golfer and pop culture icon enticed new fans to finally follow a sport that had long been mocked as painstakingly dull to watch alone. In other words, Woods not only raised his own profile through playing golf but also managed singlehandedly to raise the profile of the entire sport in the consciousness of the American people.

Tiger Woods's star rose as Major League Baseball was embroiled in an era of public scrutiny due to allegations of rampant steroid abuse among players. Additionally, the National Football League was being criticized by fans for employing several former criminals, most notably the dog-killing quarterback, Michael Vick. Amid the controversy in two of America's most beloved sports, Tiger Woods remained a positive symbol, standing in stark contrast to the boisterous and excessive reputations attributed to his athletic contemporaries. To many fans and members of the media, he was infallible. By daybreak on November 27, 2009, all of that had changed. The media frenzy that followed Woods's fateful Thanksgiving accident would have long-reaching ramifications on his public persona and the ways that he was subsequently received by admirers.

This chapter discusses the ascendance and subsequent dissolution of Tiger Woods's status as an admired symbol in the imaginary social worlds of sports fans and media consumers. Through the case study of Tiger Woods's fall from grace, I explore how celebrity "heroes" can quickly become villains in the public eye and show, through collected humor and folk narratives, precisely how the Internet has served as a hotly contested and energetic battleground of public relations. In my analysis of these responses, I demonstrate how the Tiger Woods saga provides insight into how people organize, reinforce, and protect the integrity of their imaginary social worlds through symbolic interaction and the sharing of humor in Internet contexts. Most important, I interpret the folk responses found online in the weeks and months following Woods's bizarre car accident (which ultimately led to the revelation of his numerous extramarital affairs and unstable personal life) to demonstrate that the mass media treats certain celebrity scandals as disasters, which in turn invites the kind of colorful responses that follow death and disaster and reveals symbolic expositions on the human condition.

The Beginning of the End: Tiger Woods's Crash as Impetus for Public Discourse

Shortly after 4:30 a.m. on Thanksgiving night 2009, news broke that Tiger Woods had been involved in a "serious" car accident in which he crashed his Cadillac Escalade into both a fire hydrant and a tree just outside the driveway to his Florida home.[1] Local reporters broadcasted the news that Woods was being treated at an area hospital after suffering facial lacerations and bruising from the collision, but the evidence of the airbags not deploying indicated that his vehicle had not been traveling over thirty-three miles per hour on impact. During the scramble for the complete scoop, newscasters reported that neighbors witnessed Woods's wife hitting the wrecked car with a golf club—even breaking the back window—apparently in a "heroic" effort to free him from the vehicle after striking a tree.

At first blush, some people took the story at face value as a true accident and showed ample concern for Woods's well-being. However, it was soon clear that something was "off." People began to wonder. Why was Tiger Woods out driving at 2:25 in the morning (on a holiday, no less)? How did he manage to wreck a car in his own driveway? And why did his wife need to use a golf club in order to "save" him? There were more questions than answers.

Within a matter of days, the juicy details came out: Woods and his spouse, Swedish model Elin Nordegren, had apparently been arguing before the car accident about an undisclosed family matter. She had scratched his face during the confrontation (causing the lacerations reported from the accident), which caused Woods to quickly flee his home in an attempt to evade his wife's attack with a golf club before crashing his vehicle (Cook 2009). Rumors began to surface that Woods had been under the influence of painkillers during the crash. However, the November 28, 2009, article in the *National Enquirer*—which has never been regarded as a bastion of prestigious journalism—was far more damning, alleging that the crash-inducing confrontation between Woods and his wife had been sparked by the revelation of an extramarital affair with a mistress by the name of Rachel Uchitel.[2]

Woods attempted damage control through a lackluster press conference in which he asked for privacy and decorum from the media and fans while he tended to his private family issues. No doubt to the chagrin of his public relations team, Woods's aloof delivery and defensive rhetoric only fueled outsider curiosity and riled media pundits who continued to follow the story. The story simply would not—*could not*—go away.

The public at large and the media were intrigued by the ongoing scrutiny as the full story unfolded, especially because the burgeoning allegations ran counter to Woods's reputation as one of the "good guys" in the sports world. When it was confirmed by multiple news reports that the cause of the argument that led to the accident was indeed a result of Woods's infidelity, the revered image of the indomitable golf hero quickly began to dissolve. In short order, news conduits (from blogs to broadcast television) ran updated coverage noting that Tiger Woods had indeed engaged in extramarital affairs with not one but nearly a dozen women.

By August and September 2010, several reports (including some by the *National Enquirer*) were claiming that Tiger Woods had affairs with as many as 120 women over a five-year span during his marriage. Of course, the numbers may be grossly exaggerated, but this is not the point. I bring them up here to illustrate the symbolic clout of infidelity in the discourse of reimagining Tiger Woods's public persona. The number of alleged mistresses is not significant, as they merely serve as a numerated symbol of Woods's blatant disregard for his family's welfare. These exaggerated figures also draw attention to his purportedly piggish, selfish, and thoughtless actions while skirting his responsibilities as a husband and father.[3]

Humor, Betrayal, and the Meaning of the Burgeoning Folk Response to Tiger Woods

The reportage of numerous extramarital affairs (beyond those that surfaced immediately following the car accident that sparked the news story) serves as an underhanded reminder to the public of just how scummy Tiger Woods allegedly was during his marriage, regardless of his public reckoning and efforts to reclaim his honor as an athlete and celebrity. In essence, reports of Woods's sexual conquests helped to subjugate his campaign for reacceptance into popular culture as a likeable figure while reinforcing his status as a pariah, branded by a history of unsavory psychological baggage.

Not surprisingly, many fans felt angry, betrayed, and disgusted by the scandalous details that surfaced of Woods's swanky Las Vegas hookups with exotic dancers, racy text messages to mistresses, and his bumbling attempts to cover his tracks after committing adultery.[4] The shocking contents of these news items—namely the extent of Woods's countless indiscretions—wholeheartedly debunked and destroyed the affable and wholesome persona that Woods had cultivated throughout his career as a professional golfer. The rapid loss of approval caused a social vacuum among followers and persons knowledgeable of Woods's career or iconic pop culture relevance. As a result, humorous anecdotes quickly arrived after it was evident that the Tiger Woods car crash went much deeper than the accident. In doing so, they served to ease the transition of trading a positive symbol in many individuals' imaginary social worlds (and cultural inventories) for a negative one.

Unlike a traditional mass-mediated disaster (like Hurricane Katrina) or a single, shocking event that attracts an elongated, quasi–media disaster (such as coverage on the death of Michael Jackson), the media spectacle that followed the Tiger Woods saga had to circulate and interpret the new information that was presented *immediately* upon arrival. There was no crushing impact of a single tragedy, followed by continuous coverage. Instead, the reportage of the Tiger Woods saga was very similar to the kinds of media coverage seen during the O. J. Simpson trial, which thrived off the minutia from daily court proceedings while being dramatized in the context of a gruesome back story and murder allegations against a previously respected sports celebrity. One of the major differences in the evolving folk response to the Tiger Woods story was the greater sophistication and widespread availability of the Internet as a tool of expression.[5] While early means of computer-mediated communication (such as listservs and basic e-mail applications) were available and indeed used during and after the O. J. Simpson trial for humorous expression, they were unable to connect users to a vast, ubiquitous network of information and vernacular expression in the ways that the Internet now offers users today.[6] A closer example may be found in the 2003 to 2004 media coverage of basketball player Kobe Bryant's marital infidelity and sexual assault trial (see Michaelis 2003; Johnson 2004).

Like other folk responses to major news events of the twenty-first century, the predominant method of Tiger Woods joke and narrative circulation took place via e-mail and in online discussion forums, especially in the "comments" section of news sites that reported on the evolving story as new information became available. Beyond one major example, Photoshopped humor was not a principal component of the humorous folk response to the Tiger Woods saga as it had been in the wake of 9/11 and ensuing devastation left by Hurricane Katrina. Instead, wordplay humor, golf jokes, misogynist rhetoric, and narratives about Tiger Woods became a major source of entertainment and helped to frame just how far (and how fast) Tiger Woods had fallen in the public eye.

Oral and Digital Variations on Tiger Woods Humor: Proverbs, Riddles, Photoshops, and Narratives

In retrospect, many of the jokes that entered into oral and electronic circulation during the height of the Tiger Woods scandal's media saturation (from November 2009 to February 2010) exemplify the ways in which joke tellers creatively tailor their humor and delivery toward the interpretation and recontextualization of news events as they unfold. Jokes began to appear the day after the news broke.[7] Some of the earliest jokes that appeared online use wordplay rather than the "bite" of content-driven incongruity. For example (all collected November 27, 2009—only one day after the accident took place):

> Tiger Woods crashed into a fire hydrant and a tree. He couldn't decide between a wood and an iron.

> Tiger Woods is so rich that he owns lots of expensive cars. Now he has a hole in one.

> Tiger Woods wasn't seriously injured in the crash, but he's still below par.

> Q: What's the difference between a car and a golf ball?
> A: Tiger can drive a ball 400 yards.

The jokes are punchy but not particularly cutting. If anything they poke fun at the absurdity and foolishness of the fact that Tiger Woods managed to crash his car before leaving his own driveway—a task that at first appears difficult to replicate unintentionally. The structure of the joke is in the form of a folk riddle; the narrative organization represents the survival of an accepted formula for the successful telling of a joke. In delivery, the sharp wordplay merges descriptions of terminology from Woods's profession that elicit the desired humorous effect in response to the risqué implications encoded in the prose. Above all, the jokes make light of the car crash.[8] However, as more details surfaced about the causation of the Thanksgiving night incident—namely the revelation of Woods's marital tensions and particularly the golf club attack perpetrated by Tiger's wife, Elin—the bite of the jokes stepped up a notch as well, because their rhetoric draws attention to action rather than linguistic turns (all collected November 28, 2009):

Q: What were Tiger Woods and his wife doing out at 2:30 in the morning?
A: They were out clubbing.

Q: Why did Tiger Woods's wife come after him with a 5-iron?
A: Because he really "teed" her off.

Elin has done something that [competing pro golfer] Phil Mickelson never has: beat Tiger Woods with a 9-iron.

The humor serves to turn the seriousness of the unfolding news story—the infidelity, violence, and family discord—into a pleasurable narrative. The earliest jokes in circulation made light of the car accident news story before the subsequent details of infidelity had surfaced. By contrast, the newer jokes disclose the story's new developments as evidenced by the introduction of Woods's wife into the narrative, yet they maintain the delivery dynamics of the earlier joke examples. In particular, the humor shifts its attention to the actions of Woods's wife, Elin, especially regarding her role in causing the car accident. Two examples that surfaced around December 1, 2009, were:

Q: What do Tiger Woods and a baby seal have in common?
A: They have both been clubbed in the head by Norwegians.

Q: What song does Tiger Woods have stuck in his head?
A: "Norwegian Wood."

While these jokes bring Woods's spouse to the fore, they do so in an attempt to draw connections to their audiences' cultural inventories. Simultaneously, they mock her status as a foreigner in the United States by playing off of her Scandinavian heritage, even though she is actually *Swedish* instead of the cited "Norwegian." The newer jokes reveal structural evidence of repetition and variation, mediated by the changing contexts of the news. A representative example of this comes from the lone Photoshopped image about Tiger Woods as his situation began to attract widespread circulation during the controversy. Perhaps the most popular image to appear (and ultimately "go viral") was a mock Christmas card that was playfully billed as being sent by the artistically enhanced individuals whose picture appeared on the card: a battered Tiger Woods and his slap-happy wife, Elin (see fig. 12).

The mock Christmas card was widely circulated via forwarded e-mails and the web during December 2009, purposely (and humorously) coinciding with

Figure 12. This Photoshopped image from a popularly circulating e-mail titled "Tiger Woods' Christmas Card" captures the essence of the then-burgeoning news story. By the time that this image had reached over a million views—within a matter of days from its first transmission online—the public had already begun to turn on Woods.

the time of year in which many people traditionally send holiday cards to friends and extended family that often feature a portrait of their own immediate family (Santino 1995). The holiday ritual of sending a card and family portrait to loved ones during December is also occasionally accompanied with the sending of an "update letter" that fills in recipients on the sending family's year in review (such as activities, job news, exciting revelations, etc.). E-mail appears to be replacing the physical exchange of such fodder as it is a cheaper, faster, and equally effective means of achieving the desired symbolic gesture of yearly tides and connectivity to an extended network of meaningful individuals. Nevertheless, the tradition remains viable, even if hybridized between the analog and digital mediums. An anonymous, clever (but likely amateur[9]) artist took note of this stable holiday tradition and proceeded to manipulate a regular picture of Woods and his wife in order to create an artistic output that rhetorically embodied and encapsulated the major visual and narrative markers of the news event, namely the befuddling imagery of a jilted, golf-club-toting wife, and an injured, besmirched celebrity athlete.[10]

The Photoshopped Christmas card embeds humor in the mockery of the real-life media nightmare that Tiger Woods and his family were facing. Moreover, the intentional perversion of the holiday card tradition makes light of the practice as an awkward or archaic gesture while simultaneously invoking its components in order to have an effect as a cheeky rhetorical device. Variations on the Christmas card's presentation appeared throughout the peak lifespan of the image's circulation. Other web-based folk artists modified the "original" Photoshopped image in order to adorn the couple with more festive holiday apparel, and in at least one case a variation showcased a frame surrounding the original image while printing "Merry Christmas from the Woods Family!" in vibrant colors.

Contexts, Cultural Inventories, and Traditionality in the Evolution of Woods Humor

While the earliest jokes focused on the foolishness of Tiger Woods's driveway car crash (and were accordingly aimed directly at him alone), then shifted to mock the enraged actions of his spouse, the third wave of jokes refocused their energies at Woods's actions and began to appear less than five days after the *National Enquirer* story broke (which had subsequently prompted several other mistresses to come forward). Once again, the humor tapped into the new proof of Tiger Woods's rampant adultery while mixing golf terminology, wordplay, and joke formulas for the desired humorous effect. Collected December 1–3, 2009:

A lion would not cheat, but a tiger would. [Wordplay proverb]

Q: What did Tiger Woods change his first name to?
A: Cheetah.

Q: What is Tiger Woods's handicap?
A: White women.

Q: How did Tiger Woods keep track of what hole he was on?
A: By the tattoo on her back.[11]

Like some elements of the Challenger disaster joke cycle, other riddles mock Woods's commodified connection to advertising and endorsements:

Q: What is Nike's new slogan?
A: Just did it. (Collected December 15, 2009)

Q: Who is Tiger Woods's new sponsor?
A: Durex [condoms]. (Collected December 19, 2009)

KFC is coming out with a Tiger Woods meal: it features white breasts only. (Collected January 6, 2010)

If Tiger Woods isn't careful, he's going to get GatorAIDS . . . or the "golf clap."[12] (Collected January 13, 2010)

Many of the jokes about Tiger Woods also expose insight into the joke teller's cultural inventory, which helps to explain how it informs the creative process. For example, the following joke displays an acute juxtaposition of popular culture knowledge with an edgy hook for shock and humorous value:

Q: What is the difference between Tiger Woods and Magic Johnson?
A: HIV. (Collected December 19, 2009)

The "shock" value of the insensitivity from the folk riddle is meant to surprise the audience into laughter due to its blatant and somewhat morbid thoughtlessness.

These joke examples support the incongruity theory of humor that, according to Elliott Oring (1987), suggests that jokes are predicated on the perception of appropriate social incongruities and that the appropriate incongruities are the locus of a joke's base meaning. A joke may thus carry a variety of meanings in contextual performances as derived by the motives of the joke teller (Oring 1987, 279).[13] For those who tell or listen to risqué humor, the "extreme incongruity between an expectation of what is acceptable and appropriate and the actual response" contributes to the perception of the humor's value (Bronner 1985, 43). In this case, the humorous anecdotes about infidelity demarcate Woods's behavior as inappropriate; they also project the individual joke teller's reverence for the concept of loyalty by rhetorically voicing his or her support for the concept of monogamy. Other circulating humor examples also show a structural marker of repeated, variable folklore at work, such as:

Q: What's the difference between Tiger Woods and Santa Claus?[14]
A: Santa only comes once a year. (Collected online, June 2, 2010)

The invocation of Santa Claus (in the joke setup) reveals the traditionality of the humor—not just because of the riddle formulas' accepted value as an organizational tool for delivery but also because of the usage of past oral traditions in the prose itself. A longtime Santa joke in oral tradition—Q: Why does Santa have such a big sack? A: Because he only comes once a year—is meant to be crude by playing on the words' double meanings while also serving to undermine the intended purity of Christmas proverbs and carols that also use the punch line as a narrative hook. These particular examples show the performers' awareness—be it conscious or subconscious—of past folkloric forms.

Riddle-type jokes were not the only folkloric form invoked to humorously conceptualize the Tiger Woods incident. Narrative stories were also circulated on the Internet, and they revealed repetition and variation in their content as well. The following example is actually a revision of a humorous narrative about Bill Clinton that was in circulation during and after news about the Monica Lewinsky scandal had surfaced (see Oring 2003):

The Pope and Tiger Woods died on the same day and because of an administrative mix up the Pope went to Hell and Tiger Woods went to Heaven. The Pope explains the situation to the administrative clerk in Hell, and after checking the paperwork admits that there is an error. "However," the clerk explains, "it will be 24 hours before it can be rectified."

The next day the Pope is called and Hell's staff bids him farewell. On the way up, the Pope meets Tiger Woods coming down from Heaven and they stop to have a chat.

"Sorry about the mix up," apologizes the Pope.

"No problem," replies Tiger Woods.

The Pope says, "I am really anxious to get to heaven."
Tiger asks, "Why is that?"
The Pope responds, "All my life I have wanted to meet the Virgin Mary."
Tiger smiles and says, "You're a day late." (Collected August 9, 2010)

Of course, this narrative was not the only one to be recycled from those circulating during the Clinton-Lewinsky scandal. Nevertheless, it reveals a deeper performative aura that attracts listeners to invest their time into the punch line.[15]

Tiger Woods and the Function of Humorous Expression

On page 108 of the April 2010 issue of *O, The Oprah Magazine*, in the Healthwise section, a small advice bubble discusses the benefits of gossiping, arguing that "gossiping can solidify friendships and strengthen your moral compass—so long as you're judicious about what you say and whom you say it to (dishing about Tiger Woods's latest mistress with your best friend: yes; spreading false rumors about your boss to half the office: no). Sharing juicy information with friends strengthens social bonds, and experts say gossip also informs us about what is acceptable and unacceptable behavior." Gary Alan Fine and Bill Ellis (2010) note in *The Global Grapevine* that gossiping and rumor-mongering provide "an opportunity for people and communities to explore how their nation is changing" and help to make sense of the individual's surrounding world (3). In the case of Tiger Woods, rumors and other jocular rhetoric serve not only to project and process the changing worldviews of the tellers and passers as their imagined relationship with Woods undergoes revision but also to subconsciously construct a feeling of self-superiority within the audience. In commenting on celebrity behavior, joke tellers are able to circumvent or bend the boundaries of taste by rhetorically projecting their own values and perceptions about the actions. So while it may be inappropriate to joke with coworkers about sex or genitalia, the context of a media event like the Tiger Woods scandal not only elicits performative entertainment at his expense but also opens up a playful dialogue about otherwise taboo subjects under the subconscious guise of camaraderie and relationship building.

By framing Woods's actions as deviant and repulsive, the humor reinforces socially assigned behavioral expectations and puts pressure on general conceptualizations of gender roles. Within the circulated humor, males (embodied by Tiger Woods) are rhetorically stereotyped as weak, slovenly imps who think with their genitalia. Women (embodied by Elin Nordegren) are rhetorically commended by joke purveyors for invoking a masculine, violent response to punish a partner's deviance.[16] Woods is thus symbolically castrated through the various humorous anecdotes that reference venereal disease, sexual excess, and Woods's own failure to uphold monogamy in his marriage (another sexualized psychological symbol). By removing his figurative genitalia, he is left symbolically powerless—in effect, eviscerated within the imaginary social worlds of his former followers. The transition from hero to villain becomes easier to handle. This transformative symbolic process happens with many other scandals or falls from grace.

The humorous responses to Tiger Woods's actions were not only crafted and disseminated to rhetorically punish his actions. They were also tacitly retaliating against the false character of Woods as blindly propagated by the media. Rather than accept Woods's actions as a disappointing lapse of judgment, media consumers assigned blame to the entities that endeared him to them in the first place. In the eyes of viewers, the media and its conglomerates hosting the commercial products that sought his endorsements, the sport that hosted him as their poster child, and the general glossy image that was upheld by the media as a whole were responsible. Further, media consumers' internal knowledge of the fact that Woods was in fact not a "real" friend of theirs, but an "imaginary" figure in their lives, also inflamed their reactions to his behavior. This again demonstrates how people use humor to retaliate against the emotional hegemony of the media following a disaster in that they express anger over being duped into a superficial idolization of a celebrity.

While the Tiger Woods saga may appear to stretch the definition of "massmediated disaster," I should reiterate that I am using the term in reference to any news event that attracts widespread media coverage, oversaturates media outlets, and is adopted into the folk discourse through symbolic interaction. Additionally, in this case there is a rhetorical treatment of it as disaster in references to Woods's "meltdown," "breakdown," "explosion," or "fall." Media reported the original incident as a potentially fatal accident and, afterward, as a disaster for his reputation. The slew of artistic and narrative responses to reports of Tiger Woods's infidelity exemplify how the Internet is primarily used as a simulated community where personally satisfying symbolic interaction can take place in ways that cannot always be achieved in the physical world. Additionally, the study of Tiger Woods's scandal provides another perspective on the folk response to a mediated tragedy that is not related to death but instead related to the value of living life a particular way and reaffirming certain folk values.

The Internet "preserves" folkloric material longer than oral tradition. Tiger Woods humor lodges on the Internet like a visual archive, and even though the jokes may have faded in oral circulation, websites and other forums (some static, others still dynamic) persisted in hosting Woods-related humor for a long time thereafter. While archived materials may lose their "freshness" to some folklorists seeking to understand an event's historical context, they nevertheless provide textual data from a once-potent moment of time. If collected in the process of their dissemination (as with many comments' sections to formal and informal news sites), these texts reveal much about the folk response to a particular event, as I have attempted to demonstrate here. In the next chapter, I expand on the applications of the Tiger Woods case study with an analysis of the death of Michael Jackson; in doing so, I demonstrate how celebrity deaths recontextualize the memorialization process and complicate the folk response to such events.

CHAPTER 6

Dethroning the King of Pop

MICHAEL JACKSON AND THE HUMOR OF DEATH

By any measure, Michael Jackson—"the King of Pop," "the Gloved One," "Wacko Jacko," whatever you want to call him—was a cultural icon. As the best-selling artist of all time, the complex musical and pop culture phenomenon left a tremendous legacy and a wealth of cultural reverberations from his career and sensationalized personal life after his passing in June 2009. An estimated one *billion* people witnessed the broadcast of Michael Jackson's funeral on television (Bucci and Wood 2009). In print, radio, Internet, and other media circles, Jackson accumulated an eclectic corpus of fans, enemies, critics, and colleagues who obsessed about every detail of his existence, from nuanced accounts of his eccentric personal habits to serious allegations of child sexual abuse at his Neverland Ranch. In other words, Jackson had always attracted folklore—even long before he died. The Internet provided even greater traction for vernacular expression about his celebrity persona.

The folk response to the news of Michael Jackson's death is particularly relevant for showing how the Internet plays a crucial and influential role in mediating and alleviating peoples' anxieties about death. As such, I examine how these responses indicate a folk revision of the symbolic values attached to Jackson during his life and how (through the ritual of narrative exchange and memorialization) they sought to posthum(or)usly shape the singer's legacy (see Sofka 2009). I document the various jokes and posthumous narratives pertaining to Michael Jackson, and I extrapolate the behavioral patterns of memorialization practices that surfaced in the days and months immediately following his passing. In doing so, I suggest that the psychological processes that take place after a depressing news story becomes a quasi-media disaster underscore the importance of vernacular expression for individuals who are entrenched in the media storm.

As my personal narrative from the introduction to this book suggests, "Jacko" death humor emerged on the Internet within minutes and hours following the announcement of his passing. They peaked within a week of his passing before slowly fading over several months alongside the oral renditions of Michael Jackson humor. To date, several hundred Michael Jackson death jokes have circulated, although many of the circulating Jackson jokes initially found on the Internet were often recognizable as being part of the oral traditions previously examined by humor scholars. In particular, Jackson jokes adopted the popularized and prototypical formulas seen in the aforementioned Three Mile Island, Challenger disaster, and 9/11 joke cycles, which included elements of wordplay, riddles, or the juxtaposition of commercialism within the humorous texts to trigger the notation of incongruity among audiences. Other jokes, such as one created after the assassination of John Lennon (Q: What's the only way that the Beatles will have a reunion now? A: Three bullets.) could be seen as evidence of repetition and variation—thus, *traditionality*—in jokes like "What's the only way that the Jackson 5 will have a reunion?" The answer: "Four bullets."

In death, Michael Jackson was memorialized, mythologized, and parodied in folkloric and media-initiated contexts. His collectively constructed "post-self" was shaped through carefully selected images, stories, and public vigils in a variety of outlets in order to "keep his memory alive."[1] Formally regulated media venues such as television and radio took special care to ensure that Jackson's funeral and other extended coverage of his life and death was sensitive to the contentious nature of Jackson's social reputation. Telecommunicated media typically chose to forgo reportage of the more unsavory narratives of Jackson's legal woes and instead stuck to the politically correct discourse of positive remembrance.

As Simon Bronner observes in a study comparing televised reports of a celebrity death to folkloric commentaries, television "takes on an important role in this drama as a common source of mass-cultural images and phrases" but avoids answering spectator questions that are incorporated into folk humor of the victim's interpersonal relations (1988b, 87). Bronner's study was of orally transmitted commentaries primarily among adolescents in a confined geographic region. Arguably, the Jackson joke cycle exaggerated the process he described by being globally diffused on the Internet. The Jackson cycle also took on distinctive characteristics as a form that moved back and forth between oral- and Internet-transmitted communication as a hybridized vernacular expressive pattern.

Jackson's posthumous persona was stripped from the context of formal media by consumers and subsequently broadcast throughout the folk-moderated dwellings of cyberspace. In a variety of Internet forums, websites, and blogs, Jackson became the subject of graphic lampooning or, conversely, vehement defense from supporters. In the quasi-formal venues of the Internet, such as gossip sites or other purported news sites, the protocol of reportage followed more closely that of traditional televised coverage. Most computer-mediated communication, however, often directly engaged and challenged the boundaries of good taste and contested the appropriate means of grieving, remembering, and reimagining the posthumous persona of Michael Jackson in opposition to the prescribed sentiments found on television and radio. Above all, it is important to note that the death of Michael Jackson was first reported on the Internet, and as such the cyberspace venue should serve as the starting point for a comparative examination of the rhetorical strategies employed in the amalgamation of humor that his death spawned or influenced.[2]

Mass Media and Hybridized Performance in the Folk Response to Jackson's Death

Due to his "supercelebrity" status, the folk response to Jackson's death was more pervasive and tenuous than the circulating humor about other celebrity deaths that had occurred around the same time.[3] And although many other stars may have achieved great fame and fortune, few have actually penetrated the cultural inventories of nearly every corner of the Earth in the way that Michael Jackson did. From his childhood until death, spanning over fifty years, Michael Jackson was mobbed everywhere he went, and the media attention that he garnered (both positive and negative) was scrutinized on a level only a handful of other stars could attract. So while the latest boy band sensations or teenage heartthrobs may have flocks of fans and paparazzi follow them wherever they go today, it is unlikely that they will maintain the same level of stardom for many decades to come, especially when their fans grow older and realize not only that the majority of their music is horrible but that the performers often do not individually contribute anything to their laughable "creative" outputs.[4]

Whereas numerous television programs and radio broadcasts meticulously reported on the death of Michael Jackson, the Internet managed to act simultaneously as a forum for the dissemination of news reportage and personal reactions to his death, in a sense producing a living archive of the entire event as it unfolded. Again, the imaginary, liminal space that the Internet provides acts as a conduit for the exchange of information, a meeting place for those drawn together by the perceived communal tragedy. Liminality provides psychologically protective distance by allowing users to create an emotional buffer from the seriousness of the ongoing news. The Internet's simulation of community following Jackson's passing helped to ease the acceptance of his death in a manner that also protected users from embarrassment over having an emotional reaction to the news. Furthermore, the hybridization of culture again provided guidance in navigating the emotionality of the situation at hand.

A latency period for humor is typically observed following tragedies, whereby people forgo telling jokes about the event (see Ellis 1991, 2001, 2003). However, the Michael Jackson joke cycle did not appear to yield to these social expectations in cyberspace. There are several contributing reasons that may account for why Jackson humor emerged more quickly online than other death humor that has historically followed media disasters. First, there was a pre-existing repertoire of numerous Michael Jackson jokes before his death, and in many cases their formulas—often loosely based on the motifs discussed throughout this work—were quickly recycled to cater to the news. Second, the Internet—now even more accessible and utilized than ever before—offered greater anonymity and flexibility that masked the consequences of disregarding the expected latency period. Third, the public persona of Michael Jackson was a spectacle that was mediated by cultural attraction and fascination to the multilayered ambiguities of Jackson's identity, which all at once complicated questions of race, sexual orientation, age, and even gender throughout his public career, owing in part to his ever-changing image and plastic surgery foibles, and encouraged the facilitation of folkloric speculation on his character and eccentricities (Gómez-Barris and Gray 2006; Graham-Smith 2008). But these were not the only reasons.

The public at large was naturally more curious about the postmortem identity of Jackson as a potential clue to his ambiguous physical presence; the meta-awareness of this may have sparked humor in some circles. Furthermore, the widespread suspicion of Jackson's guilt in the molestation of several boys (including a cancer patient) likely loosened social restrictions on expectations of allowing a latency period.[5] Last, and perhaps most important, popular culture observers were reeling from the death of several celebrities within a short period of time during the summer of 2009, resulting in Jackson-related death humor having a shorter latency period than typical of such events. The rash of celebrity deaths acted in two ways: the deaths psychologically perturbed the greater population, which resulted in the encouragement of new celebrity jokes to permeate for longer periods of time than previous joke cycles in order to ease the growing sense of chaos surrounding the multitude of deaths. In doing so, joke tellers and their audiences were able to relieve internal anxieties about their own mortality.

Numerous celebrity "death hoax" urban legends have circulated about the supposed demise of famous people: Paul McCartney of the Beatles was supposedly killed in a car accident (the folklore from which exacerbated a lengthy following in popular culture); actor Abe Vagoda was believed to be dead numerous times since the 1970s; child stars Fred and Ben Savage apparently met their demise in either a tragic accident or violent suicide (no one is really sure); "Mikey" from the Life cereal commercials was rumored to have consumed Coca-Cola after ingesting Pop Rocks, which resulted in his stomach exploding; comedian Sinbad was said to have died alone and broke; actor Jeff Goldblum was reported to have tragically died after falling off a cliff in New Zealand; and Oprah Winfrey was said to have recently been found dead, facedown in her apartment. These hoaxes are meant to elicit emotion and displays of concern, which are then preyed upon by knowing hoax mongers as signs of weakness or gullibility. However, beyond the "gotcha" impact of a celebrity death hoax, its function is actually quite similar to celebrity death humor—by trivializing death (especially by targeting the dichotomous usage of celebrities that are either very famous or were once famous but currently reside in obscurity), the teller of the folklore creates an emotional wedge between reality and the seriousness of the content.

The lack of death humor in cyberspace about celebrities who died close to the time of Michael Jackson likely explains why humor about Jackson's death did not yield to the established latency conventions. While the single event of Michael Jackson's passing may have constituted a "mass-mediated disaster" given the oversaturation of televised coverage about his life and death and his larger-than-life public persona, the psychological impact of numerous celebrities perishing so close to one another undoubtedly caused increased anxiety and confusion. Actors and showmen such as Dom Deluise (May 4), David Carradine (June 3), and Ed McMahon (June 23) all passed away within a month or so of each other in 2009. Their deaths began to draw attention to the growing numbers of celebrity deaths that had been taking place. In some cases jokes emerged on the Internet, but they usually appeared sparingly and were even more uncommon in oral traditions. Farrah Fawcett and Michael Jackson both passed within hours of each other on the same day (June 25), and their deaths were shortly followed by the passing of television ad spokesman Billy Mays (June 28), American football star Steve McNair (July 4), and legendary television anchor Walter Cronkite (July 17).[6]

On the Internet, death humor about celebrities who died before Michael Jackson adhered to the decorum expected of a latency period. Even jokes about actor David Carradine, who received the most news coverage after supposedly dying of autoerotic asphyxiation, did not encourage the immediate influx of online humor that Jackson spurred following his death. It is fathomable that the public collectively interpreted Michael Jackson's passing to be a part of the greater influx of celebrity deaths. Thus, while a latency period for individual Michael Jackson death humor did not appear to have existed in cyberspace on the surface, the reality is that the notion of true latency was likely blurred by the successive deaths of other high-profile stars before Jackson, which caused him to be absorbed into the latency period appropriated to members of the burgeoning "dead celebrity" folk group.

By the time of Jackson's death, the period of public decorum had already passed in the public's mind, and the acceptance of celebrity death humor was consequently more prevalent. The social tensions about celebrity death humor were already waning by the time the announcement of Jackson's death was made public. However, as a symbol of many things both good and bad, the posthumous persona of Jackson became a social piñata for the release of anxieties embodied by the rash of celebrity deaths. More specifically, the complex interpretation of Jackson—the human being—in popular culture also needed to be reconciled with the social need for closure.

Joke Types, Variations, and Meaning

Unlike oral traditions where jokesters have to account for social decorum, users in cyberspace commented more immediately and more extensively about aspects of Jackson's public persona, especially the accusations of child molestation that preceded his death.[7] Some examples of the most popular Michael Jackson jokes (collected June 25–29, 2009) that were found on message boards, forwarded e-mails,[8] and humor websites include:

Reports that Michael Jackson died of a heart attack are incorrect. In fact, he went to the children's hospital and had a stroke.

Prior to his death, Michael Jackson had requested a sea burial . . . strapped to 2 buoys.

At the time of Jacko's death he was trying to quit the Cub Scouts . . . he was down to ONE pack a day!

At the autopsy they found children's underwear strapped to Michael Jackson's upper arm. According to his doctors it is just a patch as he's been trying to quit for a while.

Michael Jackson has died from a heart attack by the age of 50. It's the first time he's been fucked by anything older than 12!

Apparently Jackson has requested in his will that his ashes be placed inside an "etch-a-sketch" . . . so even after his death, kids can continue to play and fiddle with him.

MJ's dying wish was for his body to be melted down into LEGOs. This way the kids can play with him for a change.

People are wanting MJ's coffin to be left open before they bury him so that kids can see him stiff for one last time.

These jokes appear to reveal cultural values by emphasizing the innocent playfulness of childhood as well as the abuse of that innocence. The comedic formulas conform to a socially constructed prototypical structure that challenges the accepted social conventions of political correctness following the announcement of a death. Many of them are meant not only to remind audiences of Jackson's alleged sexual abuse of minors but also to be somewhat absurdist in their presentation so as to elicit a pleasurable response from listeners. The double meaning of these examples supports the incongruity theory of humor (see Morreall 1983; Oring 1987, 2003).

It is important to emphasize that the joke tellers in the aforementioned examples (and many of the other circulating Jackson jokes) use historical contexts to make the jokes more relevant and effective for audience reception. The prior knowledge of existing allegations about Jackson's sexual abuse of children is central to understanding the joke tellers' motives and humor. On one level, the wordplay is meant to be humorous, but the central critique encoded in the jokes is further admonishment for Jackson's alleged predatory sexual behaviors by the joke tellers themselves. Gratification for the joke tellers and the audience is related to the level of awareness about the overarching themes and context of the joke topic's public and private personas as well as other social contexts, such as other celebrities' deaths or worsening health (Lamb 1994, 227).

Jokes often serve as means to test and endorse cultural values following tense events by going against the grain of expected social decorum (Ellis 2001, 8). Cyberspace makes this not only accessible but also expected. Michael Jackson was singled out for humor not only because of the opportunity for creative expression but to convey certain values about his character as well and how that character should be remembered or revered in the public's perception and memory. In serving this social function, the "folk riddle" was one of several categories or formulas of humor that emerged following Jackson's death:

> Q: What's the difference between Michael Jackson and Farrah Fawcett?
> A: About three hours. (Collected June 25, 2009)

> Q: Why did Michael Jackson die on the same day as Farrah Fawcett?
> A: He didn't want her to be the only white woman grabbing all the headlines. (Collected June 25, 2009)

Curiously, Farrah Fawcett's family and fans were angry that Jackson's death coverage completely overshadowed many public memorials and news coverage about her life and death. Still, Fawcett was not the only celebrity who was incorporated into Michael Jackson death humor:

> Q: What's the difference between Michael Jackson and the Jonas Brothers?
> A: The Jonas Brothers will be playing gigs in August. [The performer's identity varies in the joke cycles to include any popular living, actively touring (and predominantly younger and newer) musicians—common examples included Fergie, Britney Spears, or Miley Cyrus.] (Collected June 27, 2009)

> Q: What did Ed McMahon and Michael Jackson have in common?
> A: Ed always said "Here's Johnny . . ." and Michael always said "*Where's* Johnny . . . ?" (Collected June 29, 2009)

As reverberations from the abundance of celebrity deaths unfolded throughout the summer, joke tellers incorporated awareness of the health of living celebrities, such as the revelation that actor Patrick Swayze had terminal cancer. Before long, the folk riddles found on the Internet mutated into the oral telling of Jackson jokes as they related to other celebrity death humor:[9]

> Q: What are Farrah Fawcett and Michael Jackson getting for Christmas?
> A: Patrick Swayze. (Collected orally August 10, 2009[10])

Other jokes quickly emerged in the folk riddle pattern, again employing wordplay with double-meaning and contextual jokes related to elements of Jackson's public persona, both as a musician and as a figure of media scrutiny:[11]

> Q: What were Michael Jackson's last words during his heart attack?
> A: EEEEEEEEHHHHHHHHHHHHHHHEEEEEEEEEEEEEEEE!!!!!! (Collected June 25, 2009)

Q: Why did Michael Jackson go to Hell?
A: Because he was "Bad." (Collected June 26, 2009)

Q: What was the cause of Michael Jackson's death?
A: "Human Nature." (Collected June 28, 2009)

Q: What's the difference between Michael Jackson and Disney films?
A: Disney films can still touch kids. (Collected July 1, 2009)

In addition to the "folk riddle," other recognizable joke categories included rhetorical questions about his death, jokes that incorporated other celebrities or their deaths, incidental humor based on events from Jackson's music career, wordplay about Jackson's songs and lyrics, jokes about Jackson's pre- and post-mortem appearance, and especially jokes about his alleged sexual attraction to children. These jokes appeared in a variety of forums, with a substantial number arriving in the form of witty stories (Collected June 25, 2009, to July 8, 2009):

> [When] Farrah Fawcett got to heaven God said to her: "Farrah, because you have been such a good person throughout your life I will give you one wish." Farrah thought about this and replied: "God, I only want one thing and that is for the children of the world to be safe." God agreed to Farrah's wish and killed Michael Jackson.

> Toxicology report is out. It seems Michael Jackson died from an allergic reaction after eating some 12-year-old nuts. [Variations include "10-year-old wieners" as the food poisoning culprit; also, the age of the purported food items vary.]

> Madonna has paid her respects to the Jackson family—and asked how much they want for the kids . . . [Variations include "Angelina Jolie" and other celebrities who have adopted several children from around the world.]

> MJ's cardiac arrest was brought about when he found out that Boyz 2 Men were a boy band and not a delivery service. [Variations include differentiations in the cause of death, including suicide, stroke, or heart attack, among others.]

> EMTs arriving on the scene said that they could have saved Michael Jackson, but couldn't get into the driveway because it was blocked by his Big Wheels.

Again, as with other circulating jokes, context—particularly the public knowledge of Jackson's allegedly sordid or rumored past—is central to the teller and audience's satisfaction with the joke. This is especially true of jokes that integrate Jackson's lyrics and song titles into their punch lines:

There are unconfirmed reports of people hearing "Thriller" playing backwards from the morgue—Apparently he's de-composing.

As Jacko was fighting for his life in the ambulance, the doctor said, "I think we should start CPR!" The Paramedics said, "No we should start heart massage!" The Driver said, "No we should start an adrenaline drip!" Then Jacko, gasping for breath said, "You Wanna Be Startin' Something!"

There will be a post-mortem today to determine which was the cause of death: (A) Sunshine, (B) Moonlight, (C) Good Times, or (D) The Boogie.

After Michael Jackson's death, they were unsure what to put on the death certificate. In the end, one doctor pointed out that it doesn't really matter if he's "Black or White."

Michael Jackson gets to the gates of heaven and God says to him: "I cannot decide if you are black or white, so just beat it."

To all the Michael Jackson fans, when you're laying in bed tonight, as a tribute to Michael, JUST BEAT IT.

Others incorporate manipulated proverbs to commentate on Jackson's appearance:

Like Michael Jackson always said: "Live fast, die young, leave a vaguely Vietnamese looking woman's corpse."

While others joke more directly about Jackson's plastic surgery foibles:

Paramedics at the scene report that Michael Jackson never got his color back.

Early reports are that the hospital does not know what to do with the body, as plastic recycling is not collected until next Thursday.

I genuinely feel sorry for Michael Jackson's family. The decision to bury, cremate, or recycle cannot be an easy choice to make.

Of course, Michael Jackson's physical appearance was not the only target of humorous expression. Some Michael Jackson jokes that existed before his death were recycled with new meanings or additional folk commentary, such as: "MJ won't burn in Hell; he'll melt," referring to Jackson's plastic surgery, to which a commenter on an Internet message board replied: "Well, at least he has practice burning," creating a meta-joke by referencing the fact that

Jackson was severely burned during the filming of a 1984 Pepsi commercial.[12] Another folk riddle of previous oral traditions reprinted online after Jackson's death appeared:

Q: What's the difference between MJ and Casper?
A: One's white and scary, and the other's a ghost.

To which a commenter on a message board jokingly replied: "Well, I guess not anymore." Or another example that I collected on July 6, 2009:

Q: Why did Michael Jackson die at 3:15?
A: It's when the big hand touches the little hand.

In oral traditions prior to Jackson's death, this folk riddle also had a previously popular incarnation that was brought to my attention when I witnessed several commentaries surface in response to the modified version's telling at a bar in Bloomington, Indiana: "No, no—it's supposed to be 'what time did the children take a nap at the Neverland Ranch?' Then you say, '3:15; when the big hand touches the little hand.'" For the commentator, the previously existing version of the joke was the "right" one; the application of prior oral traditions to new Jackson death humor seemed incorrect, or at least confusing.[13]

Stressing the psychological motivation for generating humor (and relevant to note here), Alan Dundes and Carl Pagter assert that "stressful and traumatic events of national or international scope often stimulate the generation of new folklore—although the new folklore may turn out to be old folklore in disguise" (1991a, 303). Like the Tiger Woods narratives that invoke patterns found in Bill Clinton joke cycles, one can observe this process with a McDonald's joke that circulated following Jackson's death (which seems to suggest a linking of two icons from popular culture into symbolic equivalents):

Out of respect, McDonald's has released the McJackson burger: 50-year-old meat between 10-year-old buns. (Collected June 26, 2009) [Variations include calling the burger the "McMichael" or "The Thriller Burger," with the ages of the "buns" varying.]

The "Michael Jackson burger" jokes actually derived from a preexisting Jackson joke of the mid-1990s:

McDonald's is bringing out a new burger: the "Michael Jackson Burger" . . . It has 35-year-old meat inside 5-year-old buns. (Circulating in 1994)

This particular joke cycle (both in its original and newly imagined form) appears to be directed both at Michael Jackson, the accused pedophile, and also at McDonald's, the fast food conglomerate. The incorporation of a fast food chain into the joke supports this assertion but also underscores the consumer's awareness of commercial oversaturation by the McDonald's corporation. Thus, the joke is a rebuke of the omnipresent media coverage about Jackson's death while tacitly admonishing McDonald's for its hyperextended presence in the contested telecommunication medium, and the posthumous joke as well as the joke from the 1990s pay special attention to Jackson's age in an effort to seemingly "date" the cultural relevance of the swipe. The incorporation of commercialized elements in juxtaposition with the main tragedy-derived joke fodder is not a new phenomenon. Willie Smyth notes that by "symbolically reducing the disaster to the level of a television commercial and showing the joke tellers' ultimate dependence on media language, the jokes also reflect the degree to which people are controlled by the images broadcast over the airways" (1986, 260). In this way, joking also reaffirms the collective dissonance between the audience and the commercial hegemonic forces they are combating in their retreat to cyberspace.[14]

While there was already an existing archive of Michael Jackson jokes in circulation on several humor websites, several specialized "Jacko" death humor websites arrived shortly after Jackson's death was made public. Many of these websites housed the earliest humor about Jackson's death, and even nonspecialized joke sites began to host blogs about the circulating jokes within days of the news breaking. For example, take Yankeesdaily.com, a baseball blog site that was taken over by a single, wildly popular post on Michael Jackson jokes during the summer of 2009.[15] The site is not significant as a rhetorical text for the jokes that it hosted about Jackson's death in and of itself per se but, rather, for the tacit jockeying for social position in the response forums by users brought together by Jackson's death. Moreover, unlike its specialized, humor-oriented website brethren like deadmichaeljacksonjokes.com (which appeared less than twenty-four hours after Jackson's passing but is now defunct), the Yankees Daily blog remained as active as it was during the heightened joke dispersal period.[16] In summer 2009 it was patronized by persons who were likely unaware that such a joke database existed within its pages without a specialized search since the site returned to its original function, catering to a more generalized sports audience interested in the New York Yankees.

In examining web-based humor about former President Bill Clinton, Elliott Oring identifies six major categories of identification that can be extrapolated to organize the typical responses found on Internet humor message boards such as the one originally featured on the Yankees Daily blog: *indexical* responses, which have an authentic "voice of the people" response used to reflect mainstream attitudes); *distracting* responses, which relay the enjoyment of the joke while expressing that there is "a disjunction between the humor of the jokes and the reality to which they allude"; *tendentious* responses, which see the jokes as "aggressions and appreciate them as such"; *offensive* responses, which regard the joking as hostile and offensive; *harmless* responses, which regard the joking as simply "just jokes"—that they are basically harmless; and *perilous* responses, which warn of the consequences for partaking in joking by sharing folk wisdom that encourages appreciation or decorum for the subject of ridicule (Oring 2003, 135–37). Many of the categories outlined by Oring were readily identifiable in the earliest messages posted on the Yankees Daily blog [all text is *sic*; collected June 26 to July 3, 2009]:

> . . . that's just not funny. I love a good joke and a sick joke but that isn't either!
> Fucking hilarious. Well done all.
> This is sick. When your fucking mothers die let me make jokes about how much of a dumb bitch she was for making dumb ass kids who take the time out to make fun of a dead person and racism as well
> I think it's hillarious that people are so sensitive . . .

In all of these cases and throughout much of the site, the posted responses on the death and treatment of Michael Jackson's memorialization included a variety of participants. As Oring notes, the "individuals willing to register their opinions on the Web tend to be those with strong, well-defined views and a willingness to express them publicly" (2003, 135). This appears to be the case with the Yankees Daily blog—there were twinges of satire, genuine disgust, admonishment, and sarcasm all at war with one another. Of course, in addition to the responses that revealed the complex emotions stemming from anxiety over the death of a cultural icon (or in some cases actual celebration of the death of a "sick pedophile"), the site also acted as a conduit for posting and retelling jokes, and many of the jokes found on the site were repeated several times on the same message board thread and eventually on other sites, or imported from other sites. In the absence of jokes, there was "flaming" between posters,[17] with accusations of unoriginality or just simple critiques of peers' lack of joke-telling abilities, such as with the following example:

> Sean S [responding to another user's post]:
> Someone is a little cranky today . . . by the way, next time you try and insult me, why don't you try and use some capital letters, I hear typing in caps makes you appear cooler to your cyber-friends.

Half these jokes aren't even funny, and to be honest I laughed more at [another user's] comment than all of these jokes combined.

If you're going to insult probably the most original man alive (now dead), you need some originality. The paedophilia jokes stopped being funny in the year 2000.

What's the difference between Michael Jackson and this website?
Michael Jackson had talent and originality.

What's the difference between Michael Jackson and his tired Paedophilia jokes that have been circulating the Internet for years?
Michael Jackson died in 2009, the Paedophile jokes didn't.

Oh, and by the way, I love how you posted Michael Jackson jokes on a blog which only appears to post about baseball. I totally get the correlation between the two, considering Michael Jackson and The Yankees both love to play with balls.

This example shows the satirical and sarcastic responses that can surface in the wake of contentious death humor that mocks folk forms. The response is purposely brazen and directly challenges a previous poster's reasoning behind spreading Michael Jackson death humor, thus exerting the poster's authority over the offending commenters. "Sean S" displays his quick wit in a suddenly volatile environment; there is real bite in his words.

Many of the jokes collected about Michael Jackson show participants' awareness of his professional career and his iconic status in popular culture. Indeed, Jackson's evolution as a pop icon had two distinct phases. While he has always garnered attention for his eccentricity during his adult years, Jackson's later career was forever overshadowed by the allegations of child sexual abuse in 1993 and later in 2003. It is possible that the fans who grew to "know" Michael Jackson before these allegations (through his music, most likely) were more likely to defend his legacy online. Others, such as younger generations who came to know Michael Jackson through popular culture as a social pariah (rather than through his creative outputs) had less incentive to pay respect to social decorum, especially given the sordid nature of the alleged sexual abuse of minors. The dichotomy of folk reactions may reveal the contextual experience of Internet users and suggest a demarcation of one's status as a digital native or immigrant. In the final analysis, it is impossible to determine the social and historical contexts from which all of these folk responders operated.

The Function of Humor in the Bereavement of Celebrities

The collection of Michael Jackson humor serves as a notable example of celebrity humor about death or social deviance that the past several years have yielded in folk and popular culture. While the aforementioned examples are not exhaustive in their scope, they represent the circulating genres and meter of humor that Jackson's death invoked. More than anything, the dichotomy of congratulatory versus defensive responses to the posting of Michael Jackson death humor suggests a cultural "split" in the ways that people use the Internet to release anxiety.

Following a tragic event, there are those people who use the Internet in an attempt to simulate connectivity following a perceived communal loss through symbolic gestures of unity (by invoking proverbs or phrases) or by using the cyber venue to disrupt communal coalescence through derisive behavior. In the end, though, the desire is the same: whether gratuitous or kind in their rhetoric, people go online to feel connected to others in some way. Even those who lurk—those who do not participate themselves in online participatory culture and absorb information as silent observers—are a part of the globally connected discussion. Despite fears that the Internet would alienate individuals and keep them isolated, the folk evidence I have amassed throughout this book shows social connection in other ways besides social networking. Regardless of the means, the fact remains that cyberspace—which involuntarily connects every person with access to a modern technological device at all times—"solves" the human desire to be a part of something larger than oneself, even if it is at a subconscious level. As the humor about Michael Jackson indicates, joke tellers and their audience convey their cultural attitudes and contexts through their responses to the circulating dialogue themselves.

The passing of Michael Jackson is a particularly provocative case study of the folk response to celebrity death. In many ways, Michael Jackson's celebrity cannot be categorized in the same way as other "A-list" stars such as actors Robert Downey Jr. or Tom Cruise or "B-list" celebrities such as Gary Coleman—all of whom have garnered their fair share of mockery, teasing, or other unwanted attention throughout their careers.[18] The reaction to Jackson's death represents the extreme folk response wherein the reality of death was so unsettling that tremendous, symbolic displays of grief were present, as seen in the worldwide vigils, tributary concerts and media releases, and other forms of memorialized textual and material homage online as well as at the physical settings of significance from Jackson's life and career.

Conversely, in the absence of the grief response or the expectation of observed decorum, the extreme opposite reaction—that of dark and extreme humor—was expressed by individuals to thwart the emotional hegemony of the death event as seen in the media and also to quell the emotional weight that its reverberations caused.[19] These responses, however different in their content and audience, serve a similar purpose: to rhetorically connect with other like-minded people. Indeed, this is why celebrity culture is such a pertinent example of how people use experience to create, maintain, and idealize social relationships.

☙

CHAPTER 7

Laughing to Death

TRADITION, VERNACULAR EXPRESSION,
AND AMERICAN CULTURE IN THE DIGITAL AGE

In the United States, the notion of the "good old days" has prevailed in the popular imagination for some time. Many Americans look to the past and envision close-knit communities and neighborhood barbeques; others remark upon the moral superiority of the long-abandoned "traditional values" from days of yore, or extol past generations' physical connectivity with friends, family, and neighbors as evidence of a better time in American culture (see Bronner 1998, 2000, 2011; Cong 1994). To be sure, these memories and perceptions of the past are routinely romanticized, idolized, and mythologized in folk and popular culture as idyllic representations of desirable community life. But do they represent something more?

Sociologist Robert Putnam (1995, 2000) garnered a great deal of attention by provocatively asserting that American culture has indeed abandoned its "traditional" values and activities in favor of greater individual isolation and detachment from community interactions. More troubling, however, was his assessment that the dramatic decline in physical togetherness and civic activity has actually served to erode the health, livability, prosperity, and cohesiveness of American communities. Citing a number of corroborative statistics, Putnam concludes that a variety of factors likely contributed to the devaluation and abandonment of more traditional modes of cultural expression in America. But for Putnam, few were as culpable as mass media outlets like television and the World Wide Web (which was still taking shape at the time of his writing); he portrays them as social vortices that detrimentally lured individuals away from seeking or experiencing meaningful community engagements in a healthier, face-to-face setting. And while Putnam concedes that the television and Internet mediums are impressive in their reach and accessibility, he concludes that they cannot fully replicate any of the communicative dynamics of face-to-face communication, nor can they adequately compensate for the lost benefits of greater communal engagement (2000, 175–80, 216–46; see also Turkle 2011).[1]

In reality, Putnam's premise (as well as the general folk anxiety) that American culture has detrimentally abandoned its "traditional values" comes from an overly nostalgic and inaccurate revision of the past. The very conceptualization of "family" has undergone redefinition throughout the course of modern American history. Similarly, the valuation of physical togetherness has also undergone change, leaving behind aggrandized notions of "traditional" communities and their supposedly superior morals and customs to the popular imagination (see Coontz 2000). One's conceptualization of "tradition" or "traditional values" is inherently subjective and often more indicative of an individual's own worldview and ideals than those attributed to the popularized, symbolic pseudomemories of the good old days. Additionally, the nostalgic imagery that one associates with the past is (at least in part) informed by one's cultural inventory.

By suggesting that a return to embracing physical togetherness and civic engagement in one's community is essential to prevent Americans from becoming further alienated and detached from one another, Putnam promotes a false dichotomy. While statistics may show a decline in activity among certain kinds of civic engagement from years past, American culture has not abandoned its "traditional values." Instead, it has simply grown and adapted to the changing tides of modernity over time by providing new, adaptive ways to replicate the functions and benefits of earlier forms of interaction in a more efficient or attractive way. Like all components of folklore, the composition of tradition is formulated through a process of repetition and variation over time. And as previously noted, what makes something traditional is not the mere passage of time, but rather "continuities and consistencies through time and space in human knowledge, thought, belief, and feeling" (Georges and Jones 1995, 1).

Putnam's subjugation and dismissal of the contemporary modes of vernacular expression, civic engagement, and community involvement via technologically mediated communication manages to ignore and stifle the narrative of how and why such forms of symbolic interaction came to be preferable over in-person communal interactions as in years past. Moreover, it also undervalues how the individualistic desire to remain "self-sufficient"—rejecting the direct assistance or involvement of one's friends, family, or community in personal affairs and/or extracurricular activities in favor of isolation—emerged as a "uniquely American" character trait during the second half of the twentieth century in America, and even more significantly in the twenty-first century as the Internet continued to proliferate (Cullen 2004; see also Riesman 1950). But even in this supposedly "American" preference for self-sufficient solitude remains the essentially human need and desire for meaningful human interaction with others. While these technologically mediated expressive forums may lack the corporeality of community gatherings and family picnics, they fulfill many of the same social functions—most important, providing a semblance of connectivity with other human beings in a meaningful way.

Unlike in-person communication, the Internet appeals to people because it allows users to be "alone together," where they can connect socially while maintaining a degree of remoteness and protection through anonymity or perceptions of social distance.[2] In essence, users can be idealized "self-reliant Americans" who only need themselves while fulfilling their innate desire to connect with others. Here, too, it should be noted that connectivity holds a double meaning, both electronic and social. The compensatory value of communicating with others in times of social anxiety cannot be ignored—especially if the troubling event is promulgated by a groundswell of gratuitous media coverage. After all, the absence of intimacy with "real" people already encourages imaginary relationships and false senses of intimacy with celebrities and other public figures in service to suspending feelings of loneliness or disconnectedness.

The paradox of being "alone together" via new media technology should not be glossed over or simplified. Digital participants exploit the illusion of social distance online in order to "perform" an identity in the frame of the Internet venue. In doing so, users fulfill their desire for human connectivity while reinforcing their own admiration for the idea of the independent and self-sufficient individual. Even when participants interact with media online—be it video games, chat rooms, or posting to discussion threads—at least some part of them knows that other people are doing the same things as they are. Whether or not they visit a website with the goal of simply retrieving information for their own personal use, the fact remains that a person (who cared enough to compile the sought-after data) made it available for them online to download. Chances are, someone else is out there doing the same thing, maybe even at the same time. Surely there is some satisfaction in knowing that we are part of something larger than ourselves. So while the Internet medium may *physically* isolate us, it *cognitively* links us together into Marshall McLuhan's (1964, 1967) vision of a "global village" that operates like a collaborative central nervous system.

More than ever before, people are connecting with their friends and family in both "real" and especially virtualized Internet contexts (Baym 2010; see also

Blank 2009b). Using computer-mediated communication technology, people are organizing, cultivating, and strengthening their social networks (see Shirky 2008, 2010). Isolation is now but a physical state; and in the United States, symbolic interaction and vernacular expression is possible nearly anywhere, anytime via the Internet or mobile device. In a sense, the nostalgic allure of the "good old days" and its ideals of greater intimacy with peers *has* been recaptured through the online medium. While Americans may no longer be engaged in the same kinds of civic activities as past generations, many are clearly finding the same emotional attachment and fulfilling sense of belonging online.

Throughout the course of this book, I have examined the meanings and contexts behind the patterns of humorous responses to several mass-mediated disasters from throughout contemporary American history. These case studies reveal a great deal about modern society in the digital age, including attitudes about death, disaster, and celebrities in American culture. But more important, they also provide insights into the human condition and reveal how individuals manage to rely less on institutions and more on one another—for news, for debate, for a laugh, to protest, to let off steam, to commiserate, to partake in a meaningful symbolic gesture, for support—especially in times of social anxiety and uncertainty.

A great deal of the response to disaster or tragedy is rooted in the desire to reach a point of emotional stability and neutrality whereby the events at hand do not carry the heavy emotional burden that they did upon first impact (see Wuthnow 2010). It is human nature to attempt to make sense of a senseless situation. The folk response to disaster is partially a result of seeking control in a situation that appears chaotic, potentially fatal, or antithetical to dominant ideals (Gillin 1962). Consequently, the most pressing need for folk humor and other narratives in times of peril comes from the fact that it brings people together to engage with fellow human beings. Expressive humor confronts death through a process of desensitization and symbolic interaction. By responding to death instantaneously, users harness the new features of technology even as they consciously or unconsciously incorporate oral traditions from the corporeal world into the digital environment.

Online interactions alleviate anxiety by fostering a communicative dynamic that simulates and cognitively distances participants from their individual, corporeal isolation. Following a shocking or calamitous event, the Internet affords individuals the ability to circumvent institutional restrictions and social norms that may hinder their pursuit of emotional stimulation and interpersonal connectivity. Almost instinctively, people flock to their Facebook page or to a news site to relate their emotional feelings or experiences with others. The Internet helps to simulate—and thus stimulate—social interaction between individuals from all over the world who jointly converge in shared virtual space. Where actual and imaginary barriers once stood, people are able to now interact more freely, undeterred by the constraints of geography or other restrictive social mores.

The Internet has become a hybridized and ritualized space that hosts the symbolic contexts of participants within its virtual walls. By tapping into folkloric forms with analog precedents (including earlier technological devices), the Internet provides familiarity and accessibility to limitless information. No one has to be left in the dark. In the context of a tragedy or contentious event, the online venue serves as a symbolic place for collective rejuvenation while serving the intrinsic desires of the individual. Conversation and connectivity with others affirm that we are in fact alive and well, even if we feel wounded inside. Accordingly, folkloric expression on the Internet helps people to establish a common ground with others and reassure themselves that they will not be alone to face an unknown future by themselves.

As sociologists Peter Berger and Thomas Luckmann assert, the "most important vehicle of reality-maintenance is conversation" (1966, 152–53; see also Abrahams 1968b; Caughey 1984, 119–56). Navigating the digital world helps users to make sense of their collective experiences and commune with other humans, among the most basic of social needs. Emotional connectivity between fellow human beings is transmitted and collectively shared across the ever-blurring boundaries of space and place online. This navigation of the digitized folk system is a major component of how Americans are socialized and how both they and their digital immigrant brethren socially and emotionally connect with the outside world (see Turkle 2005). Instead of gathering a group of friends together to talk about the latest gossip or to vent frustrations about a celebrity's death, people can now paradoxically be left unbothered by familiar faces from their daily lives yet still manage to engage the whole world in a virtual, imagined space online.

The popularization of social networking sites such as Facebook have complicated the previous restrictions of imagined personal space, including issues of public and private sharing. Other applications or game-based websites (such as Facebook's social networking site for kids, Togetherville) essentially encourage and train youth to cohort online, thereby implying a socialization process into the Internet as a tradition. Nowadays, not only can children and adults alike manage crops, raise animals, and maintain a barn through the popular "Farmville" Facebook application online but they can send, create, and/or receive gifts through the medium and others like it. Some digital "gifts" even require payment to be sent. Nevertheless, the lack of physicality in a virtual "gift bear" avatar does not disqualify it as a material object as the recipient interprets and engages the digitized gesture. From a sender's perspective, the gift is meant to convey the same thoughtfulness and provide a psychological boost just as it would in a "real world" exchange, albeit in a more informal way. These tensions are again unique social hurdles facing participants in the digital age.

As Internet scholar Sherry Turkle offers: "At each point in our lives, we seek to project ourselves into the world, . . . [and] the computer offers us new opportunities as a medium that embodies our ideas and expresses our diversity" (1995, 31). It can also be said that the computer serves as our faithful companion during the hunt for news and gossip online about things that matter to us. Computer-mediated communication such as the Internet provides a means for individuals to develop tools for their own psychological well-being in the postmodern era. As people aim to project themselves into their social world, new media allows for unprecedented access to a range of simulative expressions across a limitless medium.

Given the disembodied nature of online interaction it may be easy to forget that there is nearly always a real, live human being behind every digital communication. Online, tradition can be symbolized through aesthetic or textual proclivities that frequent the domain's communicative discourse, such as the invocation of commonly used phrases or distinctive lingo, or the use of a representative tagged picture that is shared among users and assigned meaning. Thus, the "folk" web can be visual, textual, and symbolic all at once. This is the point; the Internet and modern technology are not displacing the traditions of folk culture. Instead, they are *hybridizing* expressive behavior by fusing the simulation of connectivity with the individual's psychological need to connect with others. The interactive environment online provides a virtualized rendering of analog communication dynamics—news sites are frequently organized like a slightly modified version of a "real" newspaper, for example—which, through the incorporation of aesthetic and organizational traditions derived from older analog material patterns, instills a sense of familiarity that may guide the browsing experiences of new and experienced users alike.

Folklorists Richard Bauman and Charles L. Briggs point out that tradition "has been reportedly on the verge of dying for more than three centuries" (2003, 306). Nevertheless, they offer, tradition "continues to provide useful

means of producing and legitimizing new modernist projects, sets of legis-
lators, and schemes of social inequality" (306). With the click of a button a
narrative reaches thousands—potentially millions—of people through a complex network of information diffusion facilitated by new media technology.
Community *and* tradition are both alive and well in the twenty-first century,
albeit in ways that may be unseen to the eyes of uninitiated digital immigrants
(see Jenkins 2008; Prensky 2001a, 2001b, 2004, 2006, 2007; Tapscott 1999,
2008). Technology provides the means to an end. On discussion forums,
blogs, and news sites of all stripes, participants can now add *their* views about
others' take on an event, or write their own posts—inserting their own edito-
rial opinions—while managing to engage in a productive dialogue along the
way. Their digital interactions augment or contrarily decry the sensationalist
reporting tactics of "official" or corporate media outlets that hegemonize the
emotional response to disaster.

Following a mass-mediated disaster, cyberspace becomes a venue of refuge
for the anxious public by acting as an interconnected conduit of folkloric
dissemination. Participants are empowered by the simulation of community. Some users reinforce the superiority of their ideals in conjunction with
groupthink and other rhetorical exchanges. This dynamic underscores a major
benefit of online interaction (versus face-to-face communication) for users:
it is perceived as being more egalitarian, which in turn attracts participants
wishing to circumvent corporate influences or emotionally hegemonic media
coverage. However, as rhetorician Barbara Warnick points out, the Internet
venue is not quite as autonomous or circumventive as some users may believe:

> Nineteenth- and twentieth-century theories of rhetorical influence emphasized
> the role of a text's author in crafting messages stylistically suited to the audience
> and milieu of a speech or printed text. . . . Instead, [today] they are made up of
> the efforts of programmers, designers, writers, and planners. With the exception
> of blogs and individual sites, many major Web sites with substantial audiences
> are corporately authored. . . . Critics must move away from the idea of the
> "work" and designed and authored by a single individual to the idea of the "text"
> as part of a larger system of hyperlinked and coproduced sites. . . . Not only are
> users influenced by media elements such as hyperlink patterns, display technolo-
> gies, and design elements, but they are also influenced by the content of what is
> said and how it is said in the text as written and communicated. (2007, 122)

In sum, even when users attempt to avoid corporate influence or reject the
media's attempt at emotional hegemony following a disaster, their cultural

inventories (as demonstrated by their subsequent symbolic interactions) usually reveal a detailed awareness of the very forces that they perceive as threatening. So while a full escape from corporate influence may be technically impossible (even online), the Internet nevertheless allows greater freedom for expelling one's thoughts, a perk that lends itself well after a shocking news event takes place.

Owing to the unquestionable ubiquity of the Internet in American society, it stands to reason that nearly all folklore originating in cyberspace will inevitably penetrate the boundaries of orality, and vice versa. The true difference in narrative formation and transmission between oral and electronic folklore is in the timing and context of delivery. The pseudodemocratized venue of the Internet may elicit authentic and raw responses more quickly than traditional oral forms of humor, but ultimately the sentiments expressed online will reach the physical world, with or without modification.[3] That is to say that the interchangeability of folklore, especially narratives such as jokes and urban legends, is not exclusive to either format; rather, their diffusion and the audience's perception of their origin are immaterial once they are shared. The text itself is what matters, but the context nevertheless reveals much—especially in a hybridized culture.

The transition from an analog to digital medium—which requires the shifting visual contexts of three dimensions to two dimensions—is an inherently hybridized process (see Howard 2008a; Moore, Gathman, and Ducheneau 2009). The hybridization of folk culture between analog and digital realms occurs through users' adaptation and the reinforcement of emic traditions encountered by users as they explore cyberspace. In theory, analog and digital vernacular expression begins with similar motivations. Users seek both fruitful communication as well as the reaffirmation of their own preconceived notions of acceptable social, moral, or ideological beliefs.[4]

On the flipside, the remote and disembodied physical presence in cyberspace influences some users to experiment with abrasive communication in an attempt to rile others "for fun"—perhaps like an outlaw on the American frontier. Online, people can experiment with social taboos about contentious subject matters like death or ethnicity without fear of reprisal or condemnation in their personal lives, especially if they use an avatar, screen name, or other true-identity masking tools to "smear" or textually spar with fellow Internet users (see Bronner 2009). The anonymity provided by the physical separation from peers makes the perception of social distance greater online, which often allows users to express controversial viewpoints or simply engage more openly in a dialogue with others than may be the case in the corporeal

world (Bargh, McKenna, and Fitzsimons 2002). Sounding off or acting abra-
sively in cyberspace may attract scorn or teasing in online formats—just as this
behavior may do so in the physical world—but once the user logs off and
returns to their analog domain, their social capital usually remains intact. The
Internet helps people to alleviate anxieties with others in a low-risk environment that usually cannot damage a user's credibility or social capital in their
physical lives. By blurring notions of the private and public spheres, the individual is able to reach out into ambiguous virtual terrain without consequence
and ultimately make social connections with others in a setting of perceived
intimacy (see Lieber 2010).

The online venue offers a larger platform for connecting with other individuals while still managing to provide an outlet for the user's own expressive
behaviors. More than that, it allows participants to transfer their "real world"
behavioral tendencies and needs into a simulative environment that is able
to provide faster (and possibly greater) returns on their investment of time and
energy (Bronner 2009; Jones 1997; Wehmeyer and Noonan 2009; Wojcik
2009; see also Bronner 2002, 56–64; Stallabrass 2003). Most of all, these expressive patterns suggest that "tradition" is indeed being strategically invoked
to navigate the digital landscape, both by using analog precedential correlates
for initial guidance and through subsequent, amalgamated choices that yield
a new hybrid construct. The resultant hybridization of culture serves a social
purpose beyond connectivity in a digital format; it not only helps users to navigate burgeoning social processes but also assists them in finding greater solace
and understanding of their analog lives (see Turkle 1995, 263).

In many ways, the Internet is an "electronic frontier," and one that for many
Americans seems to psychologically embody the often-mythologized "exceptional" characteristics outlined in Frederick Jackson Turner's 1893 "frontier
thesis" that are supposedly unique to U.S. citizens.[5] Of course, the Internet is
not owned nor influenced solely by Americans. However, I contend that as a
collective body of users, Americans tend to conceptualize their relationship
and general attachment to the Internet in ethnocentric terms. For these users,
the restless ambition and rugged individualism of Americans can be seen in
the entrepreneurial spirit of capitalistic, folk-moderated ventures like Craigs-
list; or perhaps in the thrill of facing danger and uncertainty while "surfing the
web" amid greater anonymity through unmonitored interaction and boundless exploration opportunities; or by invoking an outlaw's persona or vigilan-
tism, as seen in heated debates online or especially in hacker culture (McLure
2000; see also Bronner 2009; Jennings 1990). If these characteristics are truly
indicative of many Americans, the Internet can be interpreted as a limitless

virtual playground for reinforcing the superiority of the self-centric American spirit while also fulfilling social needs as a communicative outlet.

Just as Americans turned to conquering industrialization and "the machine" after the American frontier was populated, they have once again searched for a new frontier to conquer (Marx 1964). According to popular culture (namely *Star Trek*), "outer space" was to be the final frontier. However, "cyberspace" has turned out to be simply the *next* frontier of what will undoubtedly be a continued psychological process of conquering and civilizing the unknown. The frontier, like most meaningful things, is yet another symbol for optimistic, often utopian ideals. However, in the electronic frontier, new arrivals and "old-timers" come together to cultivate a true folk community that evolves with analog society (Danet 2001; Jenkins 2008, Rheingold 2000).

The digital realm is perpetually reflexive of the corporeal world, but its implications on socialization and the life course have yet to be fully explored. It is easy to see how computer-mediated communication technology is greatly influencing the ways that people now interact with one another, but it is just as easy to overlook how users' adoption of new media devices and other such technology also influences the ways in which subsequent products incorporate functions aimed at complementing user proclivities for utilizing the technology and its expressive forums. As the individual's conceptualization of tradition is the linking factor between analog and digital culture, we must also consider how the very notion of tradition is evolving owing to greater connectivity with fellow humans because of the digital age. The openness of the electronic frontier is of particular relevance here because cyber*space* symbolically transforms into a rhetorical forum for users where almost "anything goes." Participants can browse freely, unimpeded by the constraints of outside influence, and engage or avoid corporate influences however they so choose. In doing so, a binary is established between the folk and corporate web.

The praxis, or the cultural practices and processes that symbolize socially shared ways of thinking, suggests that tradition is used as an adaptive strategy in making sense of the individual's social world (Bronner 1988a, 2004). Traditions of community building and relationship maintenance are now also under revision and reconsideration because of the ubiquity of new media technology. Virtual communities are created and maintained through a process of inclusion, sharing, and other communicative engagement with both the established group members as well as new arrivals, lurkers, and passersby (see Baym 1999; Rheingold 2000, 2003). These practices represent a divergence in analog and digital patterns of knowledge sharing that also showcase how hybridization has influenced the ways that people seek out information and learn from one another. The actions attached to practices considered everyday and associated with virtualization, such as "logging on," "browsing," "surfing," and "networking," become, in fact, "traditional."

In the online realm the individual's tie to the community's tradition is psychologically amplified (see Katz et al. 2004). In contrast to oral tradition or other analog expressive interactions where information is "handed up" or "handed down" through a vertical hierarchy of information passage, the digital environment welcomes a horizontal (and seemingly democratic) means of knowledge sharing where information is "handed across" and without constraints to time, space, or context. Information retrieval is so easily accessible that it has become routinized. Thus, it is often taken for granted how the sharing of traditional knowledge is greatly influenced by mass media technology.

Indeed, the online world replicates, simulates, and virtualizes many of the familiar and pleasurable components of users' day-to-day lives as they experience it in the corporeal world—for many interacting and communicating online is easier and a more fruitful experience; for others, the Internet is just as (or even more) lonely, isolated, and devoid of meaning as "real life." However, for all of my optimism about folklore and the Internet, I would be remiss not to acknowledge the medium's downside as well, if only briefly. I do not wish to suggest that the Internet is always a happy or even a *safe* place—it can be downright depressing or scary, or used to thwart the will of the folk. Cyberterrorism, malware, pornography, the exploitation of minors, various criminal enterprises, and intricate scams can all be found in various forms online. Civil liberties and the freedom of expression can at times be impinged upon by a moderator's discretion, a hacker's interference, or the influence of institutional forces on vernacular expression. Even discussions between rational individuals can become quite dark, heated, or intense; in some cases they can even lead to violent confrontations—both in person and through rhetorical warfare. Some scholars end their analysis here, focusing instead on the negative aspects of the Internet and new media technologies while ignoring or dismissing their vast benefits altogether (see Bauerlein 2009; Carr 2011; Hindman 2008; Lanier 2011; Morozov 2011).

In spite of all the cautionary components of the web environment, I still see an overwhelming good therein. Technologically mediated communication, on the whole, makes people feel more connected with others; more informed about goings-on with peers and about world events; and as a result, they are happier. This is the *real* news. Never mind whether or not scholars disagree on the nuances of expressive behavior in online contexts, or if the online medium is a valid conduit for vernacular expression. People—our subject matter—have clearly indicated that it is! The most important task ahead is for folklorists to ignore longstanding disciplinary biases and think outside the proverbial box. As Alan Dundes once wrote, "No piece of folklore continues to be transmitted unless it means something" (1987a, vii). Folklore flourishes online in various and complex ways, repeating and varying as it disseminates because it means something to someone. Over time, it may evolve to mean something to many people. Folklorists now have a choice: stand on the sidelines as burgeoning forms of cultural expression emerge through technologically mediated means (a path that I believe could ultimately relegate the discipline to the study of antiquities), or contribute to the world's understanding of expression—in all forms—however it manifests, and embrace the study of modernity.

Afterword

PREDICTIONS ON FUTURE TRAJECTORIES OF
VERNACULAR EXPRESSION AND NEW MEDIA

Throughout the twentieth century, scholars have observed that social networks are supposedly weakest after age forty (see Brandes 1985). At this time in one's life, meaningful friendships are often diminished or dwindling, and interpersonal discord is often reported. In fact, this is such a common tale that our society has created and identified a rite of passage to facilitate the transition into "older adulthood": the midlife crisis. The ritual of the midlife crisis is often lampooned in popular culture by mocking expected behaviors— the purchasing of a "vanity item" like a fancy car, or getting hair transplants to compensate for baldness, or perhaps getting a divorce in an effort to find intimacy with younger partners. However, the ritual is most often invoked to solidify the individual's concept of friends and family in a time of internal anxiety marked by a perception of social disconnectedness. If this rite of passage is a tradition of "analog" culture, what then can we expect from the digital age in altering this cultural phenomenon? With the immense connectivity of new media technology, will future generations have any use for such a rite of passage? Or will they be *so* interpersonally connected through social networking and computer-mediated communication that the midlife crisis will fade away from our culture's psychological processing of the life course? Although the Internet is rather youth oriented (see Bronner 2009), the fact remains that today's youths will be tomorrow's middle-aged Internet users who will test the potential agelessness of social networking. Through the hybridization of behavioral forms and knowledge dissemination across analog and digital vernacular expressive venues, a new communicatory construct is created that embodies the amalgamation of behaviors across culture, regardless of analog or digital context. In this sense, "hybridization" exemplifies the intersection of repetition and variation with the shifting meanings of space, place, and context that occurs when people engage in symbolic interaction online. Throughout this process, individuals use their conceptualization of tradition to guide their actions. This notion of tradition provides an interpretative grounding, or contextual fulcrum, for how they will perceive and in turn reciprocate symbolic interactions. Essentially, tradition is used in the symbolic construction of the self (Jones 2000). Technology serves in the individual's symbolic construction of modernity, and visual cues from the digital medium capture the expressive patterns that represent dominant aesthetic ideals of the hybridized culture.

Although I contend in this book that American society has fundamentally shifted toward a preference for simulated connectivity over exclusively face-to-face interaction (through the hybridization of expressive behavior), I would like to think that the ultimate choice for how people live out their lives online is still firmly in their own control. Nevertheless, I predict that future generations will be increasingly immersed into a mass-mediated society and that as a result, the differences between analog and digital cultures will eventually be "virtually" indistinguishable.

Every future generation henceforth will inherently be composed of "digital natives." Grim and dismissive though it may seem, the fact remains that it is only a matter of time before "digital immigrants" will no longer exist, and there will be no need for a semantic distinction between the two groups. Everyone will be born into a culture where digital connectivity and pervasive social networking is the norm. We are pretty much there already, and so it will be ever increasingly important for students of folklore and cultural studies to remain engaged with the medium in order to ascertain the continued evolution of hybridized behaviors.

This prognosis may appear scary to some—especially to those who have a special reverence for "folksy" or "old-timey" stuff. I do not mean to suggest that the bucolic landscapes of America will be converted into something out of *Blade Runner* or *Minority Report* (see, there I go using my own cultural inventory to imagine a future aesthetic!). It is very likely that many of the more old-fashioned conceptualizations of folk culture will remain intact or adjust to the pressures of modernity in order to survive, much as they already have throughout history. Just as we now look to the "real world" for cues on how to interpret the digital one, so too will we again look to the past as our culture evolves. We will continue to use our notions of tradition as a guide for making sense of the world.

Like language acquisition, future generations will have the advantage of being born into a culture where an early start will yield lasting results on the learner and how they subsequently interpret their social worlds. Developing brains are more easily habituated than adult brains for the task of juggling multiple portals of social interaction and connectivity through technology (Richtel 2010). Such multitasking is now a part of the socialization process in American society. Now, more than ever, we can see concrete evidence that technology is in fact the "vital factor in the transmission of folklore" that Alan Dundes first suggested in 1977 (and hinted at long before). If five-year-olds today can text message their grandma faster than most adults who have had the technology in hand for years, imagine what lies ahead!

But more than anything, I believe that the future is exciting. I am often teased by my colleagues for such optimism regarding the possibilities afforded by Internet and new media technology. To be fair, such optimism was more of the norm around the time of the transition from Web 1.0 to Web 2.0 in the early 1990s than it is now. Some believe that there may even be an insidious element to interaction in online spaces (see Carr 2011; Lovink 2003; Morozov 2011; Zukin 2005, 269–78); they worry that the unassuming "folk" will be exploited by corporate influences as they were during the gilded age (Trachtenberg 1982). Marshall McLuhan (1964) himself warned media consumers to be wary of the manipulative power that burgeoning mediums could exude, which (given his influence even to this day) may account for the skepticism regarding digital interaction (see also P. Smith 1991, 276–77).

I may be naïve, but I believe in the folk. I believe that despite the changing tides of culture—now and in the future—we will adapt and seek out meaning in our everyday endeavors. Our values and communicative systems will shine through and prevail with integrity. Such a progression is a hallmark of the human condition, and we will continue to adapt. In the end, however different we may be—now or later—we are all part of the same social universe. While humor is often the vehicle of choice for engaging the boundless digital world in times of peril (and not, for that matter), it is actually *people* who are the true conduits of meaningful expression and their interpretation. However the future may unfold, we should never forget that this is where our study of human nature should always begin and end.

Glossary

analog (folklore): Corporeal; rooted in "real world" or nondigital interaction.

cultural inventory: The contextual frame of reference that consists of ideas, values, beliefs, and experiences (both personal and fabricated through symbolic interaction with a variety of mediums). It is a cognitive storehouse of knowledge that compartmentalizes memories and values assigned to the meaningful symbols in culture and society.

digital (folklore): Virtualized, simulated, or otherwise physically intangible expressive material that is transmitted through computer-mediated communication technology. "Digital" folklore symbolically and cognitively replicates, complements, and enhances familiar components of corporeal interactions and conventions in the discourse of interaction.

digital age: An era defined by the exponential growth of computer technology, spanning from the 1950s to the modern day. Today, it is more commonly identified with the emergence and popularity of the World Wide Web in the early 1990s and into the Web 2.0 era, with high-functioning communicative interfaces online, and with the miniaturization and greater portability of technological devices in the "real" world.

digital immigrant: Coined by education scholar Marc Prensky (2001a, 2001b), a digital immigrant is an individual who was not born into the generation that first witnessed the ubiquitous adoption of the Internet and new media technology but nevertheless adapted to the influence of such technologies by either avoiding, accepting, or adopting them. An important point to reiterate is that digital immigrants are indeed responsible for creating the technology and the communicative system that are now inseparably linked to newer generations. While seemingly pejorative as a term, "digital immigrant" is merely meant to illustrate the generational divide between younger and older technology users who were raised and socialized differently owing to the ever-increasing prominence of technology in human communication.

digital native: Coined by education scholar Marc Prensky (2001a, 2001b), a digital native is an individual who was born after 1980 and has thus been inherently subjected to the social influences of burgeoning communicative technologies throughout his or her life. The "digital native" moniker especially applies to those individuals born in the twenty-first century, as technologically mediated communication continues to progress.

dynamic (website): A type of site that is ever-changing and malleable, soliciting participation, reception, and responses in real-time. By nature, these sites facilitate interactive discourse.

emic: Research content that is consciously or subconsciously meaningful to the individual, and the informants' verbal or behavioral actions are interpreted and reported in ways that reflect an accurate "insider" perspective held by the culture or group that is being studied.

etic: The objective interpretations of a researcher; an "outsider" perspective on a cultural scene.

folk process: The means by which individuals and/or their community interpret and react to information accrual in the course of advancing their social progression or education.

folk system (online): A cultural domain that is regulated by the common practices and reinforced behavioral expectations as determined, modeled, and accepted by the people who make up the Internet community's constituency. These folk systems provide a semblance of social belonging but, more important, convey a sense of tradition within modernity.

folk web: Online participatory media, such as discussion forums and blogs, that are regulated by amateur users.

folklore: The traditional knowledge of individuals and/or their community that is acquired through oral, print, or mediated communication.

folkloristics: The academic study of folklore in a variety of social, cultural, and performative or expressive contexts.

humor: A theme of material considered to be "funny" or amusing within the context or performance in which it is transmitted to an audience.

hybrid/hybridized (folklore)/hybridization (of folklore): The blending of analog and digital forms of folklore and vernacular expression in the course of their dissemination and enactment. As a result, the distinctive characteristics and expressive forms deriving from face-to-face and online realms end up appearing (and being adopted) in *both* expressive venues. Consequently, the distinguishing characteristics of each medium are further complicated. Still, it should also be stressed that the process of hybridizing folkloric forms is always undertaken and enacted by individuals— either intentionally or outside the realm of their own awareness.

liminality: An ambivalent state of existence that is neither physical nor truly intangible.

imaginary social worlds: The network of numerous artificial, "real, but not *real*" relationships established through individuals' cognitive rapport with public figures, celebrities, and other people whom they do not know in their personal lives yet "interact with" frequently through one-way, mass-mediated outlets.

mass-mediated disaster: The result of mass media outlets—such as television, and especially the Internet and other new media technologies—providing uninterrupted, incessant, and inescapable news coverage to the point where their reportage overkill instills resentment in viewers. In response to viewers' perception of mass media's attempts at emotional hegemony, a chain reaction of narrative dissemination invades the cognitive awareness of the majority of American citizens. Often humorous, these narratives and the subsequent discourse they inspire essentially invite media viewers to consume and reproduce sentiments about the event to others quickly.

participatory culture: A culture defined by its "relatively low barriers to artistic expression and civic engagement, strong support for creating and sharing creations, and some type of informal mentorship whereby experienced participants pass along knowledge to novices. . . . Members also believe their contributions matter and feel some degree of social connection with one another" (Jenkins et al. 2009, xi). Much of the community dialogue and content of interactive forums found online constitutes components or full servicing of a participatory culture.

repetition and variation (also, "multiple variation"): The multiple existences and replications of folkloric materials across space and time. Repetition and variation may also be described as the process in which folklore incorporates new characteristics (while still maintaining or alluding to the core composition of the original source) as it disseminates beyond the contexts of its original transmission and is interpreted and reprocessed by new individuals. The evolution of this folklore can often be traced over time and thus demonstrates the traditionality of a particular body of folklore. See the introduction to Dundes and Pagter's *Work Hard and You Shall Be Rewarded* ([1975] 1978), which provides an exceptional and accessible overview of repetition and variation as it relates to technologically mediated folklore.

simulative social worlds: The patterns of community building and online vernacular expression that are forged between individuals in shared online space.

static (website): A type of site that is stable or unchanging in its display of content, such as a list, information that acts like an archive, or older personal pages from the Web 1.0 era. By nature, these sites do not facilitate interactive discourse.

Web 1.0: Spanning from the 1980s through the late 1990s and early 2000s, the Web 1.0 era of the World Wide Web consisted largely of text-based communications and interactions (such as Internet Relay Chat, "bulletin boards," and newsgroups); crudely designed, amateur personal webpages (often built from templates provided by popular hosts of free Web space, such as the now-defunct GeoCities); considerably slower Internet connection speeds (compared with the present day); and a lack of interactive capabilities or dynamic communication opportunities that would become a staple of the Web 2.0 era.

Web 2.0: A period beginning in the early 2000s in which the World Wide Web began to host increasingly sophisticated, interactive, and dynamic communicative and expressive capabilities for users. Unlike the Web 1.0 era, Web 2.0 was defined by participatory culture and greater technological sophistication. Flash video was widely available; social networking hosts like Facebook and MySpace began to develop and thrive; "Photoshopping" and other highly visualized components of expression also became increasingly available. Most significantly, greater availability and accessibility also afforded far more participation than ever before and continues today. Some experts predict that a "Web 3.0" is imminent as technology progresses further.

Notes

Preface

1. For a thoughtful overview of the folklore discipline's formation and initial aims, see Bronner (2002). For more in-depth, analytical treatments and historiographies, see Bronner (1986) as well as Abrahams (1968a); Bascom (1954); Ben-Amos (1971); Burns (1977); and Oring (1976) for paradigmatic summations of folklore throughout the twentieth century.

2. For a more expansive and critical examination of analog and digital communication from a pre-Internet, communications-centered perspective, see Wilden (1980, 155–201).

Introduction

1. A userbox is an information text box created by the moderators on Wikipedia, which is an open-source, free-access, and participatory world encyclopedia of folk knowledge available online. See Westerman (2009) for background information on the use and importance of userboxes in the Wikipedia community as well as examples of their use in practice.

2. See also Bates (2009) for an in-depth look at the statistics and how the Internet was affected by Jackson's death as well as a brief examination of the types of viral responses to the news by users in cyberspace. Of particular interest to folklorists is how the news of Jackson's death also influenced the creation of false rumors about other supposed celebrity deaths.

3. The symbolic interactions between online participants—especially on discussion forums and in virtual communities—are often perceived by users as being more democratized and capable of circumventing corporate influence. From a researcher's standpoint, however, it is nearly impossible to accurately identify the contexts that shape and inform expressive interactions observed online (at least during their immediate moments of dissemination). This is both a difficulty and an asset for the collection of

data online. A user's social context is not always clear in cyberspace, which can be problematic, but it may also heighten awareness of the intricacies of the user's textual or expressive presentations.

4. See Fisher (1987) for a more extensive and provocative theorization of narrative paradigms.

5. This is important to note because one of the major defense mechanisms in alleviating anxiety after a tragedy is denial (Wuthnow 2010, 10–12; see also Cohen 2001).

6. Baudrillard has often been criticized for his dense prose style and abstract presentation of his ideas. Therefore (in the interest of making my point clearer), I would like to invoke a reference from my own cultural inventory that I hope readers may also know: think of the film *The Matrix* (1999) and how an entire world of individuals go about their lives completely unaware of the apocalyptic "real world" that they will never know. Are their lives and experiences in "the matrix" *real* simply because their corporeal bodies exist elsewhere? See the works of philosopher René Descartes (2009; see also Almog 2005) for more on "dualism" and the "mind-body problem" from which Baudrillard derives his theoretical grounding.

7. At the time of this writing, for example, the "Tea Party" movement in American politics has been gaining steam over the last few years and has been attracting a great deal of attention for the political faction's rhetoric; strong, very conservative principles; passionate and/or angry confrontations and discourse with their representatives and fellow citizens regarding the role and nature of government; political activism; and often visceral criticism of most prerogatives supported by President Barack Obama, a Democrat. A greater examination of the movement, its core philosophies, and its impact on American culture and politics can be found in Rasmussen and Schoen (2010); for a shorter (though less ideologically balanced) treatment, see J. A. Goldstein (2011).

8. The text within these brackets represents my own addition to Davies prose in an effort to heighten its clarity.

9. "Mississippi" was replaced by "Massachusetts" in the resurgent joke, thus updating its original regional target in order to address the new accusations of racism (and temporarily renewed racial tensions) that surrounded the Gates incident throughout its portrayal in the media.

Chapter 1. Searching for Connections

1. The adoption of interchangeable parts greatly influenced and hastened the later development of the automobile and American industrialization, which had their own repercussions on the development of American society. For example, following the widespread advancement and adoption of the automobile, the newly mobile society went off driving, which led to the creation of whole industries in tourism and hotel management as well as the Eisenhower interstate system (see Belasco 1979).

2. And with regard to joke-telling, the assassination of Kennedy placed disaster jokes "on an ascending curve, . . . partly driven by the ever increasing pervasiveness of television" (Davies 2003, 20).

3. It should be noted, however, that the online venue's privilege of anonymity is not without drawbacks. Some individuals also seek to "crash" a structured, communal online scene in order to rile up participants or take advantage of the Internet venue's anonymity. "Trolling," as this behavior is called, is the deliberate act of contributing rhetorical content to a site that seeks to undermine its communal ideologies; more generally, trolling also acts in defiance of folk customs regarding communicative discourse on the Internet (such as when and where to use obscenities, for example). Individuals who partake in trolling gain pleasure from disrupting the expected discourse of a given Internet forum, and they thus have been dubbed by Internet users as "trolls" (a label that certainly encodes images of menacing creatures found in children's folklore). When an Internet user acts as a troll, they are not seeking the same kind of progressive connectivity as many of their peers but, rather, are attempting to garner attention and rhetorically announce the superiority of their opinions to those whom they are disrupting. A common adage invoked upon their appearance is "don't feed the trolls," meaning to ignore their presence. Regardless, what should be gleaned from these interactions (and their motivations) is how influential the digital format can be for fostering "real," meaningful relationships with others, both jocular and serious.

4. This may also partially explain why the digital format has been so fervently embraced as it has become available to most Americans.

5. Regular Internet usage instills a registry of aesthetic values in users (which varies, depending on the kinds of interactions routinely sought out by an individual). Such values are constantly being subconsciously acquired, reinforced, and reshaped through repeated exposure to the dominant aesthetics of the Internet. To be sure, "how and why does folklore remain stable and change?" has long been one of the three "questions that are central to folkloristics" (Georges and Jones 1995, 317). The presence of multiple variation deriving from dominant aesthetic motifs online helps to explain the broad similarities found between the sites of artists with no relation to one another beyond their shared craft. Certainly, there is no manual or official guide for artists to follow on how they should create their websites, and yet several artists' websites seem to feature many of the same components: a folksy narrative backstory, an homage to heritage or family or regional tradition in some form (usually in prose), photo galleries of their work and/or family history, news clippings or press, basic information on their region or craft, and contact information for personal or purchasing inquiries. What else could possibly explain the widespread departure from colorfully patterned backgrounds; bold, fancy texts and images; frame-based websites; or idealizations of what constituted a "professional-looking" website of Web 1.0? Clearly, aesthetic patterns emerged, were accepted as being desirable, and were then replicated through imitation until the archaic models faded away. These similar components may constitute

forms of virtual folk architecture—a concept in and of itself that is attributable to hybridization. The Internet, as an expressive medium, serves as a disembodied, digital alter ego for many artists (see Laske 1990).

6. Of course, there is still a considerable amount of ongoing debate about the effects of violent video games on human behavior, and my interpretation certainly has detractors. For examples of the predominant counterarguments, see Cantor (2000); Goldstein (1998); Kutner and Olson (2008).

7. The function is clearly identifiable in the folk responses to catastrophic losses of human life throughout the mid to late twentieth century. For example, following the "Jonestown Massacre" on November 18, 1978, in which over nine hundred people were compelled to drink cyanide-laced punch as part of a massive suicide ritual in Guyana, one popular joke that surfaced was used to diffuse tension about the event: "Why don't people tell jokes about Jonestown?" The answer: "Because the punch-line is too long" (Goodwin 2001; see also D. Jones 1985). The drink mix Kool-Aid was said to have been used, and consequently the brand has been jokingly referenced in folk culture as a euphemism for cultish behavior or blind devotion to an idea or organization by labeling the individual as "drinking the Kool-Aid." This phrase is also occasionally self-appropriated by sports fans to rhetorically indicate loyalty to their favorite teams. The incorporation of commercial products could be seen in the Challenger disaster joke cycles (as discussed in the next chapter) as well as several other tragic incidences covered in the media, such as the public suicide of politician R. Budd Dwyer (Bronner 1988b, 2009). I briefly note the appearance of commercial items in humor that circulated during the Tiger Woods scandal in chapter 4 of this work. I draw attention to these incidences to showcase the structural traditions that link them as derivatives of the same lineage.

8. The *Holocaust* miniseries actually helped to popularize the term "Holocaust," which to that point had not been widely used in American parlance. This fact conveys the growing influence of mass media on folk culture during this era.

9. For the uninitiated, a "Photoshopped image" refers to a picture that was manipulated in an effort to purposely create a new image out of the old. The term comes from the popular computer program Adobe Photoshop, which many amateur (and professional) artists use to create a variety of artistic outputs. Throughout this study I most commonly refer to Photoshopped images when describing manipulated pictures where the imposed alterations are intentionally humorous and meant to convey a message (political, rhetorical, etc.) that can be decoded by a viewer and made meaningful on the basis of shared cultural inventories and/or worldviews. See Frank (2004) for folkloristic applications and analyses of Photoshopping.

Chapter 2. Changing Technologies, Changing Tastes

1. The terms "Xeroxlore" and "photocopylore" mean the same thing (Xerox is simply a popular brand that has become synonymous with its product, much like "Kleenex"

has become synonymous with facial tissues). The terms "Xerox humor" or "photo-copied humor" refer to the predominant motifs that typify photocopylore.

2. One popular item available locally was a ceramic, nuclear reactor–shaped coffee mug with "TMI" emblazoned on its side. Also available was a large lamp featuring a base shaped like Three Mile Island's reactor towers, with "Three Mile Island" etched on its side; the lampshade contained a full-color image of Three Mile Island in its entirety. Both items were available in the months following the accident (in addition to other kinds of reactor-shaped cups and mugs) at local businesses within a thirty-mile radius of the nuclear plant.

3. Figures 3–5 are photographs I have taken of Three Mile Island–related ephemera. The materials I have photographed, as well as the permission to include these images here, is courtesy of the Archives of Folklore and Ethnography at the Pennsylvania State University, Harrisburg. My thanks for their time and kindness in sup-porting my research.

4. See Milspaw (1981, 2007) and Osif (2004) for additional context, collection, and analysis of Three Mile Island jokes from before, during, and after the accident.

5. Variations of this "What is the temperature in ____?" joke later emerged dur-ing the Gulf War conflict in 1991 and after 9/11 in regard to retaliatory bombings (see Ellis 2003, 54).

6. This is not to say that the jokes did not travel into national circles. In fact, there were jokes about Three Mile Island on the Johnny Carson show and in other regional circles when the crisis was at its peak. My point, however, is that *after* the accident left the headlines in national news circles, it reverted to being a strictly regional phenomenon.

7. Folklore and folk culture can be found in the city, the office, and on the Inter-net just as authentically and meaningfully as in "unsophisticated" contexts. There are a handful of valuable folkloristic examples that support the claim that folklore exists in various circles of engagement (elite and nonelite, folk as well as mass, etc.). See Blank (2009b); Dorson (1970); Dorst (1990); Dundes and Pagter ([1975] 1978, 1987, 1991b, 1996, 2000); especially Kirshenblatt-Gimblett (1995, 1996); Legman (1968); Untiedt (2006). Within contemporary folkloristics, the most influential work of these is likely Richard Dorson's (1970) "Is There a Folk in the City?," which is an essay that is particularly relevant for underscoring my argumentation here. For additional histor-ical contexts on the evolving debate, see Redfield (1947). For a more deliberate exam-ination of the relationship between folk and mass culture, see Dégh (1994).

8. The same was true after Pennsylvania politician R. Budd Dwyer committed suicide on live television during a press conference on January 22, 1987, only days before the one-year anniversary of the space shuttle explosion (see Bronner 1988b).

9. They are also alternatively known as "tasteless" jokes (see Oring 1995).

10. Others have interpreted it in terms of a continuation of jokes about women in the workforce (see Smyth 1986).

11. This joke was later recycled in 9/11 contexts, such as "what color were the pilot's eyes? Blue. One blew this way, one blew that way" (Ellis 2003, 45; Hathaway 2005, 33).

12. The focus on getting the "last word" remains a part of Internet discourse today as well. See Weiss (2006).

13. This joke actually originated after a helicopter landed on actor Vic Morrow while filming *Twilight Zone: The Movie* in July 1982. The original setup went: "Now we know Vic Morrow had dandruff: they found his head and shoulders in the bushes" (Gruner 1997, 142–43).

14. At the time of this writing, YouTube hosts some of these "Gimme a Light" commercials. See http://www.youtube.com/watch?v=Bodf2HYWIAY; http://www.youtube.com/watch?v=W25jk-AQXnA; http://www.youtube.com/watch?v=kbQUtcqu39M; http://www.youtube.com/watch?v=MX-z6yoiZ-Y; and http://www.youtube.com/watch?v=ECYXIDsbyxk. All accessed March 24, 2012.

Chapter 3. From 9/11 to the Death of bin Laden

1. See Van Grove (2010) for a brief synopsis on global Internet speed averages and how, as of 2010, the United States' Internet speed is now curiously declining.

2. Functionally, Web 1.0 personal webpages served as precursors to blogs, which began to emerge around 1997 and picked up steam by the end of the 1990s. During the first decade of the twenty-first century, blogs continued to develop: in functioning as a medium for rhetorical debate or symbolic interaction, in harnessing typical aesthetic and information organization patterns, and attracting millions of different people to partake in utilizing the medium for expression. In addition to being used for personal pseudo-diary purposes or facilitating a community of like-minded individuals under the umbrella of one blog site, blogs are frequently used for politics, both by individuals as well as institutions. For more in-depth treatments of blogging, including extensive histories and analytical projections for the medium's future, see Bruns and Jacobs (2006), Lieber (2010), and especially Rosenberg (2009); for a more critical interpretation of blogs and blogging culture, see Lovink (2007).

3. At times, webrings were also employed by site owners to connect with another individual who had mutual interests, or in an effort to network with like-minded individuals in the hopes of reaching a larger audience for the site and its message. For an excellent folkloristic examination of how these networking practices were used by Christian fundamentalists for networking and to partake in ritual deliberation of shared beliefs, see Howard (2011).

4. If computer-mediated communication technology continues on its current trajectory—growing exponentially every year through increased cultural penetration; perpetual improvement in usability, functionality, and accessibility/affordability; and greater user adoption—it is sure to be far more advanced, interactive, and ubiquitous than anything we can currently imagine in the Web 2.0 era. And it will probably begin to emerge in less than a decade.

5. Writing in the Web 1.0 era, communication scholar Brenda Danet (2001) concluded that the interactivity of electronic communication was fully immersive, thereby allowing individuals to perceive online experiences as simulative extensions of the self.

6. O. J. Simpson was a Hall of Fame football player for the Buffalo Bills from 1969 to 1977 (and the San Francisco 49ers from 1978 to 1979). In 1994, the bodies of Simpson's ex-wife, Nicole Brown, and her boyfriend, Ron Goldman, were found brutally murdered as the result of multiple stab wounds to the head and neck. Simpson was charged with the homicide, but before turning himself in to authorities, he released several rambling statements to the media that hinted he was suicidal. While authorities were trying to peacefully detain Simpson both to ensure due process and for his own protection, O. J. Simpson and a friend slipped off in a white Ford Bronco, culminating in a now-infamous slow-speed police chase, where Simpson held a gun to his head while contemplating his eventual surrender to the police. As a result of Simpson's preexisting notoriety as a football player and television/film personality, his trial was a legendary media spectacle, which naturally prompted the creation and dissemination of humor. Unsurprisingly, many of the jokes about O. J. Simpson were spawned in part by the trial's accompanying media circus. For humorous materials collected during the trial, see Lamb (1994). It should be noted that prior to the 1994 murder allegations, Simpson was a generally well-liked celebrity; he had even begun to fashion a movie career for himself in the years before the trial. However, after his acquittal, Simpson was radioactive and was largely viewed with suspicion and even spite by some individuals.

7. Princess Diana perished in a horrific car accident on August 31, 1997, and many of the jokes that became popular following her death were heavily drawn from the patterns and formulas of the Challenger disaster joke cycle—just with updated punchlines to account for the new tragedy. For example, Q: What was the last thing to go through Princess Diana's mind? A: The dashboard (instead of using "Christa McAuliffe" and "The control panel" in the Q and A, respectively). For a thoughtful survey and analysis of the circulating death humor pertaining to Princess Diana, see Davies (1999).

8. Columbine humor was sparse, especially because of the fact that children were involved and Americans had never before witnessed such a violent and tragic story like that of "loner" students Eric Harris and Dylan Klebold, who brutally shot and killed twelve students and a teacher and injured twenty-one others before committing suicide themselves. However, some dared to challenge decorum and posted jokes sparingly on newsgroups like the popular Rec.Humor.Funny (now online as netfunny.com). One joke in particular drew on the conventions of a popular form of online humor in circulation around that time: textual spoofs using the formula and narrative structure/meter of MasterCard's "Priceless" commercials. Indeed, the "Priceless" joke model had developed into a full-fledged folk tradition online over time (see Frank 2011, 128–37). A surviving Columbine joke, playing off the joke formula, went: 200 rounds of ammo: $70 / Two ski masks: $24 / Two black trench coats: $260 / Seeing the expression on

your classmates' faces right before you blow their heads off—priceless. / There are some things money can't buy, for everything else there's MasterCard (Rec.Humor .Funny Newsgroup Archives 1999; for a variation of [essentially] this same joke, see Frank 2011, 129). For a punchy overview of the events that occurred during the Columbine massacre, as well as an examination of the media's response to Columbine and the influence of popular culture in the subsequent national discussion, see Plasketes (1999).

9. While not explicitly disaster or tragedy related, it bears noting that the two biggest sources of Internet humor during the 1990s were President Bill Clinton and especially First Lady Hillary Clinton. For explanation, analysis, and examples, see Horowitz (2008); Frank (2011, 31–34, 42–57); Oring (2003, 129–40); Thomas (1997).

10. See Ellis (2001, 2003).

11. For a compelling international perspective on 9/11 humor and its dissemination and reception overseas, see Csaszi (2003) and Kuipers (2002, 2005, 2011).

12. To this end, see Hathaway (2005, 45) and also Frank (2004).

13. The consequential phrase formula "if X does [or doesn't] ____, then the terrorists win" circulated widely after 9/11, and while initially used for serious purposes or to affirm symbolic displays of patriotism (almost with proverbial reverence), the saying was eventually employed to mock the more cumbersome government demands made in the name of homeland security. For example: "If you don't allow the TSA [Transportation Security Administration] to put a flashlight up your ass . . . then the terrorists win." It later became highly personalized; for example, "If you don't make me a sandwich right now . . . then the terrorists win."

14. An archived transcript of one of the Pakistani men's Twitter chronological updates during the raid can be accessed at http://tweetlibrary.com/damon/osamaraid livetweets.

15. This humorous tactic was also used after the BP oil spill took place, when a fake "BP Public Relations team" started posting "updates" on the company's progress with stopping the massive oil spill that plagued the Gulf Coast region for months. Indeed, many intentionally (and openly) fake Twitter accounts are in existence today for the very purposes of rhetorical mockery and other forms of playful humor.

16. This was also prevalent in the nonvisual jokes in circulation. For example, "It's a bird! It's a plane! It's . . . oh shit, it IS a plane!" not only required the audience to know details of the attacks on the World Trade Center (in order to understand the punchline) but also required knowledge of the correlating origin and the emulated delivery meter drawn from the Superman comic book series and the related media associated with it.

Chapter 4. "Intimate Strangers"

1. For the record, George Washington never chopped down a cherry tree. See Dorson (1976) for a lengthy study on fakelore.

2. Consumerism and commodification are important pieces of the celebrity culture puzzle; however, my specific research is more interested in the construction of imaginary relationships than the nuances of commodification and its implications. Consequently, I have chosen to refrain from distracting ruminations on consumer culture. That said, Zukin (2005) provides an accessible look into consumer culture; the context provided by Marshall (2006) is also helpful in cementing my argumentation here.

3. Note the first-name basis or nicknames attributed to celebrities like "J-Lo," "Jacko," "Oprah," "Fergie," "A-Rod," "The Biebs" (for horrendous pop star Justin Bieber), etc.

4. This claim assumes that the reader is not a celebrity. If the reader is a celebrity, please go away and stop ruining my analysis ☺.

5. This again points to my thesis that people use the Internet to symbolically connect with others in a meaningful, intimate way as they compensate for a lack of connectivity in their "real" lives.

6. See chapter 6.

7. While many fans would likely state that they are just supporting their team by wearing a jersey, diehard fans often appear to be subconsciously fantasizing about playing the sport themselves or even "taking over" for the athlete as if they were the same person. Grant McCracken (1988, 1989) productively writes about a process called "displaced meaning" wherein people attain cultural ideals through acts of consumption. For McCracken, it is not just an individual act of intimacy when a person wears a favorite player's jersey—that person is simultaneously communicating to others his or her identification with the player's values through rhetorical expression.

8. I should clarify that the term "imaginary social world" was coined by anthropologist John Caughey in 1984. "Simulative social worlds," by contrast, is a term that I have coined here to better articulate (and distinguish) the nature of online vernacular expression and the relationships that are derived from such interaction.

Chapter 5. From Sports Hero to Supervillain

1. It should be noted that the first broadcast about Woods's car accident appeared just over two hours after the actual event in question took place (at 2:25 a.m., according to police records). By daybreak, the story had hit the Internet and was widely distributed across the globe. The information chain that was created in response to the incident continued to send its assembly line of facts through the vast network of mass media outlets at the disposal of citizen journalists, formal media members, and interested info seekers throughout the height of the story's lifespan.

2. Rachel Uchitel had previously been linked to a 2008 affair with television actor David Boreanaz during his wife's pregnancy. Her second appearance as an alleged celebrity mistress also raised the stakes of the news reportage, and many bloggers quickly predicted that the salacious *National Enquirer* would be the recipient of a defamation lawsuit in short order if they did not produce "actual proof" of their allegations about

Woods. See http://www.nationalenquirer.com/celebrity/67747 for the original *National Enquirer* (2009) report.

3. That said, I should clarify that I am not passing judgment on Woods's behaviors—regardless of my own personal dislike for his actions—but rather I am seeking to channel the overarching sentiments expressed by many people whom I encountered in my ethnographic collections online and in person.

4. For example, a rambling voicemail was leaked to the press in which Woods requested that a mistress delete his name and text messages from her phone because he suspected that his wife had caught wind of their affair. The audio evidence gave additional credence to the swirling accusations and provided concrete proof—straight from Tiger's own mouth—that there was a darker side to his personality that many of his followers never knew existed.

5. Another obvious (but important) difference is that O. J. Simpson was accused of gruesomely murdering his wife and her boyfriend, whereas Tiger Woods was accused of adultery. The seriousness of the respective allegations is important to consider: Simpson was acquitted of committing murder but remained a social pariah who never resumed his work in sports broadcasting or acting after the trial (this may also be attributed to the fact that many people judged him to be guilty anyhow). Woods, on the other hand, was able to eventually return to golf after going on hiatus for a while. By fall 2010, his reintegration into the good graces of the public eye was slow, but by summer 2012, Woods was again making the rounds on numerous national golf tournaments (albeit without demonstrating his previous level of dominance over opponents).

6. To conceptualize the vast difference of sophistication between Web 1.0 and Web 2.0, I like to use the analogy of home music entertainment's technological advancement. Vinyl LP record technology progressed into eight-track technology, which was then followed by cassette tapes and eventually compact discs, laser discs, and later digital mp3s. Each iteration was more sophisticated and compact than its predecessor, while simultaneously managing to enable greater memory storage in a single device for prolonged, uninterrupted user enjoyment. Nevertheless, each of these devices served the same function: playing music. While an old record player provides the same great music as its successors, it is commercially undesirable because it is clunky and awkward, and the sound quality is usually inferior to the advanced formats. Similarly, Web 1.0 had the same function and a similar appearance to Web 2.0, but the latter is exponentially more intricate and accessible (yet affordable) and has attracted greater patronage that continues to develop and advance the global network it facilitates. For an applied, illustrative example of Web 1.0 vernacular expression and how it contrasts to Web 2.0 technology, see McNeill (2009).

7. This assertion runs counter to the astute claims of Bill Ellis (2001) regarding the observance of a latency period following a media disaster. Ellis characterizes the latency period as a brief stretch of time (usually about two weeks) in which sobriety and decorum is consciously upheld in opposition to the allure of tasteless humor

performance, particularly during the days immediately after a serious event has taken place. However, as I discuss in the next chapter on Michael Jackson's death humor, the socially sanctioned "appropriate time" for humor to surface in the wake of a tragedy is wholly contextual; more important, the length varies depending on the nature of the media disaster and the individual needs of the narrative purveyor. Increasingly, the latency period appears to be prematurely truncated owing to the opportunities for anonymous expression in numerous online forums, which allows for risk-free vernacular expression without the constraints or expectations of defined social order. Furthermore, the observance of a latency period does not appear to be expected in the case of celebrity scandal.

8. It should be noted that part of the acceptability for the general, light Tiger Woods humor that surfaced the day after the crash was likely due to the fact that joke tellers and audiences were aware that Woods was in stable health and not critically injured as had been initially feared. Had Woods perished in the crash, it is likely that a period of shock and decorum would have instituted some adherence to a latency period (see note 7), but it is impossible to know how the remainder of the saga would have unfolded in this particular case.

9. I make this claim for several reasons. First, I can observe from my own familiarity with using the Photoshop program that the mock Christmas card's manipulated alterations are unpolished and rather unsophisticated in terms of technical difficulty to edit and splice. Secondly, I have observed numerous artists who participate in friendly online virtual community Photoshopping competitions or message boards that have been established to challenge participants to compete and most convincingly and deceptively blur the lines of visual reality and user-generated modifications with a single image. Among these die-hard Photoshop users, a consensus of dismissal and rejection has been apparent in their commentarial responses to the Tiger Woods Christmas card's popularity. In their eyes, the apparent level of difficulty for replicating such work is so miniscule that many of these participating artists write off the popular Photoshop as amateur rubbish that lacks the craftsmanship or necessary depth to be considered "art." Several artist bloggers whom I observed characterized the popular Christmas card image as being so amateurish that "a 5-year-old could make it" and grumbled that the picture was an embarrassing attempt at manipulating a clean image. Admittedly, I found it peculiar that the bloggers I observed appeared to be more annoyed by the underdeveloped artistic nuances than interested in the image's encoded humorous message. I am no elitist, but these informants most certainly are— between their headstrong disapproval of the Photoshop's novice aesthetic components and my own analysis of the image's complexity, I reckon that my assertion holds up. For an excellent overview on folklore and Photoshopping, see Frank (2004).

10. Note, also, that the Photoshopped image appears to take on the aesthetic "feel" and organization of the classic painting "American Gothic." In raising this similarity, I admit that I may be guilty of reading deeper into the image than the original, anonymous creator may have intended.

11. Often referred in the folk lexicon as a "tramp stamp," a woman's lower back tattoo is frequently mocked as "trashy" body ornamentation. In this application, the joke also rhetorically refers to Tiger Woods' choice of sexual partner as being promiscuous or "easy."

12. For compelling evidence on the traditionality of this particular example, see Dundes and Pagter (1996, 332) for examples that show its derivations from the AIDS joke cycles of the 1980s and 1990s in photocopylore.

13. Prior to the more generalized acceptance of incongruity theory in modern humor studies (post-Freud), Plato's "superiority theory" was one of the oldest and most longstanding theories of laughter and humor. Plato posited that what makes a person laughable is self-ignorance and that the proper object of laughter is human evil and folly (1992, 452). The laughable person, then, is "the one who thinks of himself as wealthier, better looking, more virtuous, or wiser than he really is" (Morreall 1983, 4). Plato's central thesis held that laughter had a malicious element associated with the derision of our inferiors. Humor could thus be used to "put someone in their place" by establishing that their wit was not as superior as their peers' via public admonishment. Plato warned against the dangers of laughter as inciting reckless abandon and even went so far as to recommend that literature "be edited to delete mention of gods or heroes being overcome with laughter" as not to show weakness or folly (Provine 2000, 13).

14. Another variation, playing on the news story and tradition of wordplay humor, went: Q: What's the difference between Tiger Woods and Santa Claus? A: Santa stops at three ho's.

15. Structuralists may note that this continuity potentially points to an organic tradition in narratives, suggesting a continuing transmission. The riddle-joke structure signals a short-lived joke "fad" related to the frame of a "sick" or "gross" joke. My thanks to Simon Bronner for pointing this out to me.

16. See Pope and Englar-Carlson (2001) for insights on the social perceptions that equate violent behaviors with masculinity. Also, for an excellent analytical overview of masculine traditions and their construction in folklore and society, see Bronner (2003).

Chapter 6. Dethroning the King of Pop

1. According to Keith F. Durkin, the postself is "the reputation and influence that an individual has after his or her death" (2003, 47) or that continues to exist in the memories of the minds of the living. This often takes place in commercial or performative ways, such as with Elvis impersonators or commodified images of Che Guevara on T-shirts. In the case of Michael Jackson, this took place in the form of humor sharing, the public broadcasting of Jackson's funeral and homage videos to his music career, the reinvigoration of Michael Jackson memorabilia, and the advertisement for the posthumous release of Michael Jackson's "This Is It" tour documentary. For additional research on the memorialization process and its social/psychological functions,

see Clark and Franzmann (2006); Dobler (2009); Field and Filanosky (2010); Foot, Warnick, and Schneider (2005); Grider (2001); Hess (2007); Jorgensen-Earp and Lanzilotti (1998); Romanoff and Terenzio (1998); Santino (2005); Vickio (1999).

2. TMZ.com broke the news of Michael Jackson's death on June 25, 2009, at 6:20 p.m. (PDT), and had already alerted readers of EMTs arriving at Jackson's residence before other news outlets had done so. The instantaneity of the Internet circumvented the hindrances that the physical publication of a "late edition" newspaper would have caused. This reality is a frequent causation for the Internet's ability to "scoop" print media.

3. The "supercelebrity" moniker that is assigned to Jackson in this chapter is my own doing; it should be noted that the term has not been used to describe celebrities of Jackson's stature in other cultural studies scholarship. I have introduced the term here to distinguish Jackson's legacy and persona from the ranks of other popular celebrities.

4. This is not always the case, of course . . . just usually. And for the record (lest I sound like a cranky jerk), I am not an ex–boy band reject hurling insults out of spite over lost glamor; I just happen to think that it is good fun to lampoon and mock the delirium of teeny bopper culture. As a consequence, I am fairly confident that fate will ensure that I have a daughter someday.

5. The truth is that society is understandably unforgiving in cases of child molestation, especially given the prevalence of sexual assaults against minors (an unsettling one in seven children are victimized). Even in prisons, child molesters (often called "Chesters" or "Cho-Moes") are ostracized and are particularly vulnerable to being attacked.

6. By the end of August 2009, Michael Jackson's death was ruled a homicide, and an investigation of a potential accidental death due to prescription drug complications was pending. I do not wish to disregard this information, but it is important to note that this reality was unbeknownst to the public at the peak of the humor's dissemination in July 2009. As such, while factually relevant to understanding Jackson's death in totality, the cause of death is immaterial to a proper discussion of the humor that Jackson's death influenced and how the Internet mediated this process.

7. Considering the sexual and aggressive overtones found in the majority of popular humor, this was to be expected. See Baker and Bronner (2003).

8. See Frank (2009) and Kibby (2005) for excellent discussions of how folklore is transmitted and shaped by e-mailed dissemination.

9. See Mechling (2002) for a review of how popular culture influences and is influenced by folk culture. This is particularly relevant in considering the transition of humor from electronic to oral formats and the hegemonic processes at work that are in conflict with folk interests.

10. Note that this joke was collected orally in August, after over a month and a half had passed since Jackson died. As this chapter argues, oral and electronic humor do not always adhere to the same latency period constraints, and the fact that jokes did

not emerge in oral traditions until over a month had passed shows that time must pass for the same level of insensitivity found more immediately online to be carried out in the physical world. It is also important to note that this joke was recycled from Princess Diana joke cycles.

11. Many of the examples are reminiscent of the folk riddles about the Challenger disaster (and other media disasters of the late 1980s and 1990s) that were recycled or modified before and after the event in oral traditions, as discussed in chapter 2—for example, Q: What was the last thing to go through Christa McAuliffe's mind? [or in other cycles John F. Kennedy Jr., Princess Diana, Budd Dwyer, etc.] A: The cockpit; her teeth; her ass, etc. Refer to chapter 2 of this book, and see also Bronner (1988b), Oring (1987), Simons (1986), and Smyth (1986) for further analysis of the folk riddle in these contexts and cycles.

12. Interestingly enough, one of the jokes about this incident—Q: What kind of shampoo does Michael Jackson use? A: Head and Smoulders [sic] (Smyth 1986, 259)—circulated before the motif was again employed more notoriously in the Challenger disaster joke cycle; however, it appeared after the joke originated in reaction to the helicopter-related death of actor Vic Morrow in 1982, as discussed in chapter 2.

13. As a note on my ethnographic experience, when I collected Michael Jackson jokes orally I also observed a wide variety of reactions that evolved as more time passed following his death. Some people were very upset that I was asking if they had heard any Michael Jackson jokes immediately after hearing that he died, commenting that it was "too soon," or that I was "an insensitive prick," as one person commented. During my ethnographic fieldwork on the streets of Bloomington, Indiana, another person actually took my phone and ran off with it, refusing to return it until I promised not to ask anyone else for jokes (granted, that took place at a bar in a college town . . . on a weekend evening). The mood lightened considerably after several weeks had passed and I was able to collect numerous jokes, most of which overlapped with the humor that I had found online.

14. Robert Dobler (2009) fruitfully explores how teens respond to the death of loved ones by mourning online through social networking sites like MySpace. His examples provide additional context on the response to grief in the digital age.

15. A direct link to the popular blog posting was formerly at http://www.yankees daily.com/?p=7573 (last accessed August 31, 2009). However, upon testing the URL in February 2012, I learned that the Yankees Daily blog was now defunct and no longer available online, even in archived form.

16. Many of the specialized websites for Michael Jackson death humor "sold out," and are currently analogous to a cyber ghost town. The material is static, irrelevant, or simply nonexistent. In many cases, the old URLs are swamped with ads and viruses, making their former appearance and function a distant memory to visitors.

17. "Flaming" is akin to verbal dueling in an online setting and is a form of trolling. The practice is found in public cyberspace forums such as message boards or a blog's comments section.

18. This terminology is indicative of a folk hierarchy that has permeated popular culture. An "A-List" celebrity is one who is featured in mainstream, popular, and desirable entertainment venues. "B-List" celebrities, by contrast, are often lampooned as has-beens or simply less talented or desirable entertainers.

19. The connection between the death of Elvis Presley and Michael Jackson is an appropriate one. In an effort to memorialize as well as fictionalize and reject the reality of Elvis's untimely death in August 1977, many fans and performers subsequently became full-time "Elvis impersonators" (see Carroll 2005; Fraser and Brown 2002; Spigel 1991). This is not to say that Elvis impersonators did not exist before his death, as they most certainly did; the same can be said for Michael Jackson impersonators. My point is that their respective deaths *did* act as a performative catalyst by attracting a greater swell of performers into the effort of public memorialization. Just as Michael Jackson was lampooned in some venues while celebrated in others, Elvis's death also garnered jokes about his weight, health, or drug abuse amid a lively public spectacle of grief. The collective cultural loss was dually noted on both sides of the response spectrum.

Chapter 7. Laughing to Death

1. Putnam may be excused for his premature and incorrect dismissal of the Internet's then-burgeoning expressive capabilities (though he *did* have his critics at the time of publication; most notably, see Ladd 1999). Since 2000, the Internet has grown in leaps and bounds, and it is no exaggeration to state that the web of Putnam's 1995 and 2000 research is a relic by comparison to the dynamic possibilities now available to Internet users (as I have discussed throughout the course of this book). New media, in particular, offers plenty of examples of computer-mediated forms of social activism and performative interactions that are coordinated online and enacted in the "real" world (see Rheingold 2003; for more direct examples and applications, see McNeill 2012). Nevertheless, there are still naysayers; unfortunately, some of them are folklorists. Bill Ivey (2011), for example, offers a depressingly backward assessment of the Internet's communicative and expressive capabilities in transmitting and/or generating authentic folklore that is eerily similar to Putnam's logic penned around the turn of the century (in particular, see Ivey 2011, 15). On the bright side, many folklorists have either already embraced the Internet medium or appear to be coming around to accept its ability to facilitate the dissemination of vernacular expression and various forms of genuine folklore.

2. My depiction of Internet users being "alone together" while communicating with others online is actually adopted from Internet scholar Sherry Turkle's (2011) book of the same name. I think that "alone together" is a rather eloquently simple and accurate way of succinctly conceptualizing the nature of online interaction. In the majority of my own research on the genres of folklore on the Internet, the variations of rhetoric in online interactions, and even the blogs and websites that have come to

constitute a genuine virtual community (see Rheingold 2000), I have consistently observed evidence that the Internet medium—despite its limitations and drawbacks—is a positive and equally viable locus of authentic symbolic interaction as face-to-face settings. Many behaviors and cultural practices have clear analogues between corporeal and virtual performative settings and contexts (see Bronner 2009). To me, "alone together" does not have a negative connotation whatsoever; I see it merely as an accurate descriptor of how many Americans prefer to go about harnessing the allure of the "good old days" in their own, unique ways while embracing the technology and cultural realities of the present day. That said, Turkle and a handful of other scholars who research technology and culture do not agree with my cheery assessment and actually see the act of being "alone together" as a troubling indication of growing alienation and communal disconnectedness within American society.

3. See Dégh and Vázsonyi (1975) and Dégh (1997) for the definitive explanations of multi-conduit theory and how folklore is disseminated through conduits that shape their content and forms.

4. An important consideration that should not be lost here is that while such social exercises are at work, there is always the possibility of one's mind being changed. People, social as they are, may revise their values or beliefs to conform to the majority, or because of meaningful experiences that alter their line of thinking, or because a logical counterpoint is introduced that causes them to reevaluate their position. What I am getting at here is that the contextual "social baggage" is not fixed and can change in response to new social pressures or stimuli. However, I would argue that such change would be indicative of an individual's immense desire for connectivity (such as a person who becomes alienated by their narrow inclusivity or one who updates their behaviors or ideologies to match a lover's) that outweighs their loyalty to their original positions.

5. In his thesis, Turner (1893) argues that Americans' perpetual advancement into the frontier exemplified the spirit of a unique people, noting "that coarseness and strength combined with acuteness and acquisitiveness; that practical inventive turn of mind, quick to find expedients; that masterful grasp of material things; . . . that restless, nervous energy; that dominant individualism" were distinguishable characteristics and distinctive qualities of an exceptional nationalist cohort. For additional insights into this thesis, as well as Turner's other important works, see Turner (1961), a posthumous compilation.

References

Abrahams, Roger D. 1968a. "Introductory Remarks to a Rhetorical Theory of Folklore." *Journal of American Folklore* 81 (320): 143–58.

———. 1968b. "A Rhetoric of Everyday Life: Traditional Conversational Genres." *Southern Folklore Quarterly* 32:44–59.

Abrahams, Roger D., and Alan Dundes. 1969. "On Elephantasy and Elephanticide." *Psychoanalytic Review* 56 (2): 225–41.

Aldred, B. Grantham. 2010. "Identity in 10,000 Pixels: LiveJournal Userpics and Fractured Selves in Web 2.0." *New Directions in Folklore* 8 (1/2): 6–35.

Almog, Joseph. 2005. *What Am I? Descartes and the Mind-Body Problem.* New York: Oxford University Press.

Baker, Ronald L., and Simon J. Bronner. 2003. "'Letting Out Little Jack': Sex and Aggression in Manly Recitations." In *Manly Traditions: The Folk Roots of American Masculinities,* edited by Simon J. Bronner, 315–50. Bloomington: Indiana University Press.

Bargh, John A., Katelyn Y. A. McKenna, and Grainne M. Fitzsimons. 2002. "Can You See the Real Me? Activation and Expression of the 'True Self' on the Internet." *Journal of Social Issues* 58:33–48.

Barrick, Mac E. 1972. "The Typescript Broadside." *Keystone Folklore Quarterly* 15: 27–38.

———. 1980. "The Helen Keller Joke Cycle." *Journal of American Folklore* 93:441–49.

———. 1982. "Celebrity Sick Jokes." *Maledicta: International Journal of Verbal Aggression* 6:57–62.

Barth, Gunther. (1980) 1982. *City People: The Rise of Modern City Culture in Nineteenth-Century America.* New York: Oxford University Press.

Barton, Michael. 1998. "Journalistic Gore: Disaster Reporting and Emotional Discourse in the *New York Times,* 1852–1956." In *An Emotional History of the United States,* edited by Peter N. Stearns and Jan Lewis, 155–72. New York: New York University Press.

Bascom, William. 1954. "Four Functions of Folklore." *Journal of American Folklore* 67: 333–49.

Bates, Claire. 2009. "How Michael Jackson's Death Shut Down Twitter, Brought Chaos to Google . . . and 'Killed Off' Jeff Goldblum." *Daily Mail Online* (UK), June 26. http://tinyurl.com/Bates2009. Accessed November 19, 2009.

Baudrillard, Jean. 1995. *Simulacra and Simulation*. Translated by Sheila Faria Glaser. Ann Arbor: University of Michigan Press.

Bauerlein, Mark. 2009. *The Dumbest Generation: How the Digital Age Stupefies Young Americans and Jeopardizes Our Future (Or, Don't Trust Anyone Under 30)*. New York: Tarcher.

Bauman, Richard, and Charles L. Briggs. 2003. *Voices of Modernity: Language Ideologies and the Politics of Inequality*. Cambridge: Cambridge University Press.

Baym, Nancy K. 1993. "Interpreting Soap Operas and Creating Community: Inside a Computer-Mediated Fan Culture." *Journal of Folklore Research* 30:143–77.

———. 1995. "The Performance of Humor in Computer-Mediated Communication." *Journal of Computer Mediated Communication* 1 (2). http://jcmc.indiana.edu/vol1/issue2/baym.html.

———. 1999. *Tune In, Log On: Soaps, Fandom, and Online Community*. Thousand Oaks, CA: Sage Publications.

———. 2010. *Personal Connections in the Digital Age*. Malden, MA: Polity Press.

Belasco, Warren J. (1979) 1997. *Americans on the Road: From Autocamp to Motel, 1910–1945*. Baltimore: Johns Hopkins University Press.

Ben-Amos, Dan. 1971. "Toward a Definition of Folklore in Context." *Journal of American Folklore* 84:3–15.

Bendix, Regina. 1997. *In Search of Authenticity: The Formation of Folklore Studies*. Madison: University of Wisconsin Press.

Bennett, Sue, Karl Maton, and Lisa Kervin. 2008. "The 'Digital Natives' Debate: A Critical Review of the Evidence." *British Journal of Educational Technology* 39 (5): 775–86.

Berger, Peter, and Thomas Luckmann. 1966. *The Social Construction of Reality*. New York: Anchor Books.

Blank, Trevor J. 2007. "Examining the Transmission of Urban Legends: Making the Case for Folklore Fieldwork on the Internet." *Folklore Forum* 37 (1): 15–26. https://scholarworks.iu.edu/dspace/handle/2022/3231.

———. 2009a. "Toward a Conceptual Framework for the Study of Folklore and the Internet." In *Folklore and the Internet: Vernacular Expression in a Digital World*, edited by Trevor J. Blank, 1–20. Logan: Utah State University Press.

———, ed. 2009b. *Folklore and the Internet: Vernacular Expression in a Digital World*. Logan: Utah State University Press.

———. 2009c. "Fieldwork, Memory, and the Impact of 9/11 on an Eastern Tennessee Klansman: A Folklorist's Reflection." *Voices: The Journal of New York Folklore* 35 (3/4): 23–27.

———. 2009d. "Moonwalking in the Digital Graveyard: Diversions in Oral and Electronic Humor Regarding the Death of Michael Jackson." *Midwestern Folklore* 35 (2): 71–90.

———. 2010. "Cheeky Behavior: The Meaning and Function of 'Fartlore' in Childhood and Adolescence." *Children's Folklore Review* 32:61–85.

———, ed. 2012. *Folk Culture in the Digital Age: The Emergent Dynamics of Human Interaction.* Logan: Utah State University Press.

Boorstin, Daniel. (1958) 1974. *The Americans: The Democratic Experience.* New York: Vintage Books.

———. (1961) 1987. *The Image: A Guide to Pseudo-Events in America.* New York: Vintage Books.

Booth, Paul. 2008. "Rereading Fandom: MySpace Character Personas and Narrative Identification." *Critical Studies in Media Communication* 25 (5): 514–36.

Brandes, Stanley H. 1985. *Forty: The Age and Symbol.* Knoxville: University of Tennessee Press.

Bronner, Simon J. 1985. "'What's Grosser Than Gross?' New Sick Joke Cycles." *Midwestern Journal of Language and Lore* 11:39–49.

———. 1986. *American Folklore Studies: An Intellectual History.* Lawrence: University Press of Kansas.

———. 1988a. "Art, Performance, and Praxis: The Rhetoric of Contemporary Folklore Studies." *Western Folklore* 47:75–101.

———. 1988b. "Political Suicide: The Budd Dwyer Joke Cycle and the Humor of Disaster." *Midwestern Folklore* 14:81–90.

———. 1995. *Piled Higher and Deeper: The Folklore of Student Life.* Atlanta: August House Publishing.

———. 1998. *Following Tradition: Folklore in the Discourse of American Culture.* Logan: Utah State University Press.

———. 2000. "The American Concept of Tradition: Folklore in the Discourse of Traditional Values." *Western Folklore* 59 (2): 143–70.

———. 2002. *Folk Nation: Folklore in the Creation of American Tradition.* Wilmington, DE: Scholarly Resources Books.

———, ed. 2003. *Manly Traditions: The Folk Roots of American Masculinities.* Bloomington: Indiana University Press.

———. 2004. *Grasping Things: Folk Material Culture and Mass Society.* Lexington: University Press of Kentucky.

———. 2009. "Digitizing and Virtualizing Folklore." In *Folklore and the Internet: Vernacular Expression in a Digital World*, edited by Trevor J. Blank, 21–66. Logan: Utah State University Press.

———. 2011. *Explaining Traditions: Folk Behavior in Modern Culture.* Lexington: University Press of Kentucky.

———. 2012. "The Jewish Joke Online: Framing and Symbolizing Humor in Analog and Digital Culture." In *Folk Culture in the Digital Age: The Emergent Dynamics of*

Human Interaction, edited by Trevor J. Blank, 119–49. Logan: Utah State University Press.

Brown, Roger William, and James Kulick. 1977. "Flashbulb Memories." *Cognition* 5 (1): 73–99.

Bruns, Axel, and Joanna Jacobs, eds. 2006. *Uses of Blogs*. New York: Peter Lang Publishing.

Brunvand, Jan Harold. 2001. "Folklore in the News (and Incidentally, on the Net)." *Western Folklore* 60 (1): 47–76.

Bryant, Clifton D., ed. 2003. *The Handbook of Death and Dying*. Thousand Oaks, CA: Sage.

Bucci, Paul, and Graeme Wood. 2009. "Michael Jackson RIP: One Billion People Estimated Watching for Gold-Plated Casket at Memorial Service." *Vancouver Sun*, July 7.

Burns, Thomas A. 1977. "Folkloristics: A Conception of Theory." *Western Folklore* 36:109–34.

Campbell, W. Joseph. 2003. *Yellow Journalism: Puncturing the Myths, Defining the Legacies*. Westport, CT: Praeger.

———. 2006. *The Year That Defined American Journalism: 1897 and the Clash of the Paradigms*. New York: Routledge.

Cantor, Joanne. 2000. "Media Violence." *Journal of Adolescent Health* 27 (2): 30–34.

Carr, Nicholas. 2011. *The Shallows: What the Internet Is Doing to Our Brains*. New York: W. W. Norton.

Carroll, Patty. 2005. *Living the Life: The World of Elvis Tribute Artists*. Burlington, VT: Verve Editions.

Caughey, John. 1984. *Imaginary Social Worlds*. Lincoln: University of Nebraska Press.

Ceruzzi, Paul E. 2003. *A History of Modern Computing*. 2nd ed. Cambridge, MA: MIT Press.

Clark, Jennifer, and Majella Franzmann. 2006. "Authority from Grief, Presence and Place in the Making of Roadside Memorials." *Death Studies* 30 (6): 579–99.

Cohen, Stanley. 2001. *States of Denial: Knowing About Atrocities and Suffering*. Malden, MA: Polity Press, 2001.

Cong, Dachang. 1994. "The Roots of Amish Popularity in Contemporary U.S.A." *Journal of American Culture* 17 (1): 59–66.

Cook, John. 2009. "How Tiger Woods Spent Thanksgiving: A Re-Cap of His Car Crash Story So Far." *Gawker*, November 30. http://tinyurl.com/TigerWoodsThanksgiving. Accessed September 15, 2010.

Coontz, Stephanie. 2000. *The Way We Never Were: American Families and the Nostalgia Trap*. New York: Basic Books.

Correll, Timothy Corrigan. 1997. "Associative Context and Joke Visualization." *Western Folklore* 56 (3/4): 317–30.

Couldry, Nick, Andrea Hepp, and Fredrich Kotz, eds. 2009. *Media Events in a Global Age*. New York: Routledge.

Couts, Andrew. 2011. "Osama bin Laden Death-Raid Tweeted by Accident." *Digital Trends*, May 2. http://www.digitaltrends.com/international/osama-bin-laden-death -raid-live-tweeted-by-accident/. Accessed May 10, 2011.

Csaszi, Lajos. 2003. "World Trade Center Jokes and Their Hungarian Reception." *Journal of Folklore Research* 40 (2): 175–210.

Cullen, Jim. 2002. *The Art of Democracy: A Concise History of Popular Culture in the United States*. New York: Monthly Review Press.

———. 2004. *The American Dream: A Short History of an Idea That Shaped the Nation*. New York: Oxford University Press.

Cwynar, Christopher. 2010. "Dear John: On the Meta-Celebrity's Misguided Attempt to be Clever." *Antenna: Responses to Media and Culture*, February 19. http://blog.com marts.wisc.edu/2010/02/19/dear-john-on-the-meta-celebritys-misguided-attempt -to-be-clever/. Accessed September 18, 2010.

Danet, Brenda. 2001. *Cyberpl@y: Communicating Online*. New York: Berg.

Davies, Christie. 1999. "Jokes on the Death of Diana." In *The Mourning for Diana*, edited by Tony Walter, 253–68. New York: Berg.

———. 2002. *The Mirth of Nations*. New Brunswick, NJ: Transaction.

———. 2003. "Jokes That Follow Mass-Mediated Disasters in a Global Electronic Age." In *Of Corpse: Death and Humor in Folklore and Popular Culture*, edited by Peter Narváez, 15–34. Logan: Utah State University Press.

———. 2011. *Jokes and Targets*. Bloomington: Indiana University Press.

Dégh, Linda. 1994. *American Folklore and the Mass Media*. Bloomington: Indiana University Press.

———. 1997. "Conduit Theory/Multiconduit Theory." In *Folklore: An Encyclopedia of Beliefs, Customs, Tales, Music, and Art*, edited by Thomas A. Green, 142–44. Santa Barbara, CA: ABC-CLIO.

Dégh, Linda, and Andrew Vázsonyi. 1975. "The Hypothesis of Multi-Conduit Transmission of Folklore." In *Folklore: Performance and Communication*, edited by Dan Ben-Amos and Kenneth Goldstein, 207–52. The Hague: Mouton.

Del Tredici, Robert. 1980. *The People of Three Mile Island*. New York: Random House.

Descartes, René. 2009. *Meditations on First Philosophy: In Which the Existence of God and the Distinction of the Soul from the Body Are Demonstrated*. Charleston, SC: CreateSpace.

Dixon, Wheeler Winston. 1999. *Disaster and Memory: Celebrity Culture and the Crisis of Hollywood Cinema*. New York: Columbia University Press.

Dobler, Robert. 2009. "Ghosts in the Machine: Mourning the MySpace Dead." In *Folklore and the Internet: Vernacular Expression in a Digital World*, edited by Trevor J. Blank, 175–93. Logan: Utah State University Press.

Dorson, Richard M. 1970. "Is There a Folk in the City?" *Journal of American Folklore* 83 (328): 185–216.

———. 1976. *Folklore and Fakelore: Essays Toward a Discipline of Folk Studies*. Cambridge, MA: Harvard University Press.

Dorst, John. 1990. "Tags and Burners, Cycles and Networks: Folklore in the Telectronic Age." *Journal of Folklore Research* 27 (3): 179–90.

"Duct and Cover: Terrorism Preparedness Guide (Ready.gov Parody)." 2003. *About.com Political Humor*, February 28. http://politicalhumor.about.com/library /blductandcover.htm. Accessed March 11, 2012.

Dundes, Alan. 1971. "Folk Ideas as Units of Worldview." *Journal of American Folklore* 84:93–103.

———. 1979. "The Dead Baby Joke Cycle." *Western Folklore* 38 (3): 145–57.

———. 1980. "Who Are the Folk?" In *Interpreting Folklore*, edited by Alan Dundes, 1–19. Bloomington: Indiana University Press.

———. 1987a. *Cracking Jokes: Studies of Sick Humor Cycles and Stereotypes.* Berkeley, CA: Ten Speed Press.

———. 1987b. *Parsing Through Customs: Essays by a Freudian Folklorist.* Madison: University of Wisconsin Press.

———. 1999. *Holy Writ as Oral Lit: The Bible as Folklore.* Lanham, MD: Rowman and Littlefield.

Dundes, Alan, and Thomas Hauschild. 1983. "Auschwitz Jokes." *Western Folklore* 42 (4): 249–60.

Dundes, Alan, and Carl R. Pagter. (1975) 1978. *Work Hard and You Shall Be Rewarded: Urban Folklore from the Paperwork Empire.* Bloomington: Indiana University Press.

———. 1987. *When You're Up to Your Ass in Alligators: More Urban Folklore from the Paperwork Empire.* Detroit: Wayne State University Press.

———. 1991a. "The Mobile SCUD Missile Launcher and Other Persian Gulf Warlore: An American Folk Image of Saddam Hussein's Iraq." *Western Folklore* 50 (3): 303–22.

———. 1991b. *Never Try to Teach a Pig to Sing: Still More Urban Folklore from the Paperwork Empire.* Detroit: Wayne State University Press.

———. 1996. *Sometimes the Dragon Wins: Yet More Urban Folklore from the Paperwork Empire.* Syracuse, NY: Syracuse University Press.

———. 2000. *Why Don't Sheep Shrink When It Rains? A Further Collection of Photocopier Folklore.* Syracuse, NY: Syracuse University Press.

Durkin, Keith F. 2003. "Death, Dying, and the Dead in Popular Culture." In *Handbook of Death and Dying*, edited by Clifton D. Bryant, 43–49. Thousand Oaks, CA: Sage.

Ellis, Bill. 1991. "The Last Thing Said . . . The Challenger Disaster Jokes and Closure." *International Folklore Review* 8:110–24.

———. 2001. "A Model for Collecting and Interpreting World Trade Center Disaster Jokes." *New Directions in Folklore* 5. https://scholarworks.iu.edu/dspace/handle /2022/7195. Accessed July 10, 2009.

———. 2003. "Making a Big Apple Crumble: The Role of Humor in Constructing a Global Response to Disaster." In *Of Corpse: Death and Humor in Folklore and Popular Culture*, edited by Peter Narváez, 35–82. Logan: Utah State University

Press. Earlier version published in *New Directions in Folklore* 6 (2002). https://schol arworks.iu.edu/dspace/handle/2022/6911.

Emery, Edwin. (1972) 1978. *The Press and America: An Interpretive History of the Mass Media.* 4th ed. Upper Saddle River, NJ: Prentice-Hall.

Field, Nigel P., and Charles Filanosky. 2010."Continuing Bonds, Risk Factors for Complicated Grief, and Adjustment to Bereavement." *Death Studies* 34 (1): 1–29.

Fine, Gary Alan. 1988. "Dying for a Laugh: Negotiating Risk and Creating Personas in the Humor of Mushroom Collectors." *Western Folklore* 47 (3): 177–94.

———. 1992. *Manufacturing Tales: Sex, Money, and Contemporary Legends.* Knoxville: University of Tennessee Press.

———. 2001. *Difficult Reputations: Collective Memories of the Evil, Inept, and Controversial.* Chicago: University of Chicago Press.

Fine, Gary Alan, and Bill Ellis. 2010. *The Global Grapevine: Why Rumors of Terrorism, Immigration, and Trade Matter.* New York: Oxford University Press.

Fine, Gary Alan, and Bruce Noel Johnson. 1980. "The Promiscuous Cheerleader: An Adolescent Male Belief Legend." *Western Folklore* 39 (2): 120–29.

Fischer, Henry W. 1994. *Response to Disaster: Fact Versus Fiction and Its Perpetuation.* Lanham, MD: University Press of America.

Fisher, Walter. 1987. *Human Communication as Narration: Toward a Philosophy of Reason, Value, and Action.* Columbia: University of South Carolina Press.

Foot, Kirsten, Barbara Warnick, and Steven M. Schneider. 2005. "Web-based Memorializing after September 11: Toward a Conceptual Framework." *Journal of Computer-Mediated Communication* 11 (1). http://jcmc.indiana.edu/vo111/issue1/foot.html.

Foote, Monica. 2007. "Userpicks: Cyber Folk Art in the 21st Century." *Folklore Forum* 37 (1): 27–38.

Foster, Michael Dylan. 2012. "Photoshop Folklore and the 'Tourist Guy': Thoughts on the Diamond Format and the Possibilities of Mixed-Media Presentations." *New Directions in Folklore* 10 (1): 85–91.

Frank, Russell. 2004. "When the Going Gets Tough, the Tough Go Photoshopping: September 11 and the Newslore of Vengeance and Victimization." *New Media & Society* 6 (5): 633–58.

———. 2009. "The Forward as Folklore: Studying E-Mailed Humor." In *Folklore and the Internet: Vernacular Expression in a Digital World,* edited by Trevor J. Blank, 98–122. Logan: Utah State University Press.

———. 2011. *Newslore: Contemporary Folklore on the Internet.* Jackson: University Press of Mississippi.

Fraser, Benson P., and William J. Brown. 2002. "Media, Celebrities, and Social Influence: Identification with Elvis Presley." *Mass Communication and Society* 5 (2): 183–206.

Freud, Sigmund. (1905) 1960. *Jokes and Their Relationship to the Unconscious.* New York: W. W. Norton.

Georges, Robert A., and Michael Owen Jones. 1995. *Folkloristics: An Introduction.* Bloomington: Indiana University Press.

Gillin, John P. 1962. "Theoretical Possibilities of Induced Sociocultural Collapse." In *Man and Society in Disaster,* edited by George W. Baker and Dwight W. Chapman, 385–404. New York: Basic Books.

Goetzmann, William H. 2009. *Beyond the Revolution: A History of American Thought from Paine to Pragmatism.* New York: Basic Books.

Goffman, Erving. 1974. *Frame Analysis: An Essay on the Organization of Experience.* New York: Harper Colophon.

Goldstein, Jared A. 2011. "Can Popular Constitutionalism Survive the Tea Party Movement?" *Northwestern University Law Review Colloquy* 105:288–99.

Goldstein, Jeffrey, ed. 1998. *Why We Watch: The Attractions of Violent Entertainment.* New York: Oxford University Press.

Gómez-Barris, Macaerna, and Herman Gray. 2006. "Michael Jackson, Television, and Post-Op Disasters." *Television and New Media* 7:40–51.

Goodwin, Joseph P. 2001. "A Supplemental Update to: Unprintable Reactions to All the News That's Fit to Print: Topical Humor and the Media." *New Directions in Folklore* 5. https://scholarworks.iu.edu/dspace/handle/2022/7198.

Gournelos, Ted, and Vivica Greene, eds. 2011. *A Decade of Dark Humor: How Comedy, Irony, and Satire Shaped Post-9/11 America.* Jackson: University Press of Mississippi.

Graham-Smith, Greg. 2008. "Habeas Corpus: Bodies of Evidence and Performed Litigiousness—the Spectacle of Michael Jackson's Trial." *Communicato* 34 (2): 278–89.

Grider, Sylvia. 2001. "Spontaneous Shrines: A Modern Response to Tragedy and Disaster." *New Directions in Folklore* 5. https://scholarworks.iu.edu/dspace/handle/2022/7196.

Gruner, Charles R. 1997. *The Game of Humor: A Comprehensive Theory of Why We Laugh.* New Brunswick, NJ: Transaction.

Hafner, Katie. 2001. *The Well: A Story of Love, Death, and Real Life in the Seminal Online Community.* New York: Carroll and Graf.

Hafner, Katie, and Matt Lyon. 1998. *Where Wizards Stay Up Late: The Origins of the Internet.* New York: Simon and Schuster.

Hatch, Mary Jo, and Michael Owen Jones. 1997. "Photocopylore at Work: Aesthetics, Collective Creativity and the Social Construction of Organizations." *Studies in Cultures, Organizations, and Societies* 3 (2): 263–87.

Hathaway, Rosemary V. 2005. "'Life in the TV': The Visual Nature of 9/11 Lore and Its Impact on Vernacular Response." *Journal of Folklore Research* 42 (1): 33–56.

Healy, David. 1997. "Cyberspace and Place: The Internet as Middle Landscape on the Electronic Frontier." In *Internet Culture,* edited by David Porter, 55–69. New York: Routledge.

Hess, Aaron. 2007. "In Digital Remembrance: Vernacular Memory and the Rhetorical Construction of Web Memorials." *Media, Culture & Society* 29 (5): 812–30.

Hindman, Matthew. 2008. *The Myth of Digital Democracy*. Princeton, NJ: Princeton University Press.

Hine, Christine. 2000. *Virtual Ethnography*. Thousand Oaks, CA: Sage.

Horowitz, Jason. 2008. "The Hillary Haters." *GQ*, January. http://www.gq.com/news -politics/newsmakers/200712/president-hillary-clinton. Accessed August 12, 2011.

Hounshell, David A. 1985. *From the American System to Mass Production, 1800–1932: The Development of Manufacturing Technology in the United States*. Baltimore: Johns Hopkins University Press.

Howard, Robert Glenn. 2008a. "Electronic Hybridity: The Persistent Processes of the Vernacular Web." *Journal of American Folklore* 121:192–218.

———. 2008b. "The Vernacular Web of Participatory Media." *Critical Studies in Media Communication* 25:490–512.

———. 2010. "Hybrid." In *Folklore: An Encyclopedia of Forms, Methods, and History*, edited by Tom Green, 682–84. Santa Barbara, CA: ABC-CLIO.

———. 2011. *Digital Jesus: The Making of a New Christian Fundamentalist Community on the Internet*. New York: New York University Press.

Inglis, Fred. 2010. *A Short History of Celebrity*. Princeton, NJ: Princeton University Press.

"Internet World Stats." 2010. http://www.internetworldstats.com/top20.htm. Accessed October 28, 2010.

Ivey, Bill. 2011. "Values and Value in Folklore (AFS Plenary Address, 2007)." *Journal of American Folklore* 124 (491): 6–18.

Ivory, Karen. 2007. *Pennsylvania Disasters: True Stories of Tragedy and Survival*. Guilford, CT: Globe Pequot.

Jenkins, Henry. 2006. *Fans, Bloggers, and Gamers: Exploring Participatory Culture*. New York: New York University Press.

———. 2008. *Convergence Culture: Where Old and New Media Collide*. New York: New York University Press.

Jenkins, Henry, Ravi Purushotma, Margaret Weigel, Katie Clinton, and Alice J. Robison. 2009. *Confronting the Challenges of Participatory Culture: Media Education for the 21st Century*. Cambridge, MA: MIT Press.

Jennings, Karla. 1990. *The Devouring Fungus*. New York: W. W. Norton.

Johnson, Kirk. 2004. "Prosecutors Drop Kobe Rape Case." *New York Times*, September 2. http://www.nytimes.com/2004/09/02/national/02kobe.html. Accessed August 9, 2011.

Jones, David R. 1985. "Secondary Disaster Victims: The Emotional Effects of Identifying Human Remains." *American Journal of Psychiatry* 142:303–7.

Jones, Kevin T., Kenneth S. Zagacki, and Todd V. Lewis. 2007. "Communication, Liminality, and Hope: The September 11th Missing Person Posters." *Communication Studies* 58 (1): 105–21.

Jones, Michael Owen. 1997. "How Can We Apply Event Analysis to 'Material Behavior,' and Why Should We?" *Western Folklore* 56 (3/4): 199–214.

———. 2000. "'Tradition' in Identity Discourses and an Individual's Symbolic Construction of Self." *Western Folklore* 59 (2):115–40.

Jorgensen-Earp, Cheryl R., and Lori A. Lanzilotti. 1998. "Public Memory and Private Grief: The Construction of Shrines at the Sites of Public Tragedy." *Quarterly Journal of Speech* 84 (2): 150–70.

Kapchan, Deborah A. 1993. "Hybridization and the Marketplace: Emerging Paradigms in Folkloristics." *Western Folklore* 52 (2): 303–26.

Kapchan, Deborah A., and Pauline Turner Strong. 1999. "Theorizing the Hybrid." *Journal of American Folklore* 112 (445): 239–53.

Kassovic, Julius. 1981. "I'm OK—You're Nuked." Paper presented at the American Studies Association Eighth Biennial Convention, Memphis, TN, November 1.

Katz, James E., Ronald E. Rice, Sophia Acord, Kiku Dasgupta, and David Kalpana. 2004. "Personal Mediated Communication and the Concept of Community in Theory and Practice." In *Communication Yearbook 28*, edited by P. Kalbfleisch, 315–71. Mahwah, NJ: Lawrence Erlbaum.

Kearl, Michael C. 1989. *Endings: A Sociology of Death and Dying.* New York: Oxford University Press.

Kennedy, Randall. 2003. *Nigger: The Strange Career of a Troublesome Word.* New York: Vintage Books.

Kibby, Marjorie. 2005. "Email Forwardables: Folklore in the Age of the Internet." *New Media & Society* 7:770–90.

Kirshenblatt-Gimblett, Barbara. 1995. "From the Paperwork Empire to the Paperless Office: Testing the Limits of the 'Science of Tradition.'" In *Folklore Interpreted: Essays in Honor of Alan Dundes*, edited by Regina Bendix and Rosemary Levy Zumwalt, 69–92. New York: Garland.

———. 1996. "The Electronic Vernacular." In *Connected: Engagements with Media*, edited by George E. Marcus, 21–66. Chicago: University of Chicago Press.

———. 2003. "Kodak Moments, Flashbulb Memories: Reflections on 9/11." *TDR: The Drama Review* 47 (1): 11–48.

Kuipers, Giselinde. 2002. "Media Culture and Internet Disaster Jokes: Bin Laden and the Attack on the World Trade Center." *European Journal of Cultural Studies* 5 (4): 450–70.

———. 2005. "'Where Was King Kong When We Needed Him?' Public Discourse, Digital Disaster Jokes, and the Functions of Laughter after 9/11." *Journal of American Culture* 28 (1): 70–84.

———. 2011. "'Where Was King Kong When We Needed Him?' Public Discourse, Digital Disaster Jokes, and the Functions of Laughter after 9/11." In *A Decade of Dark Humor: How Comedy, Irony, and Satire Shaped Post-9/11 America*, edited by Ted Gournelos and Vivica Greene, 20–46. Jackson: University Press of Mississippi.

Kutner, Lawrence, and Cheryl Olson. 2008. *Grand Theft Childhood: The Surprising Truth About Violent Video Games and What Parents Can Do.* New York: Simon and Schuster.

Ladd, Everett Carll. 1999. *The Ladd Report*. New York: Free Press.

Laineste, Liisi. 2003. "Researching Humor on the Internet." *Folklore: Electronic Journal of Folklore* 25:93–97.

Lamb, Chris. 1994. "The Popularity of O.J. Simpson Jokes: The More We Know, the More We Laugh." *Journal of Popular Culture* 28 (1): 223–31.

Langlois, Janet L. 2005. "'Celebrating Arabs': Tracing Legend and Rumor Labyrinths in Post-9/11 Detroit." *Journal of American Folklore* 118 (468): 219–36.

Lanier, Jared. 2011. *You Are Not a Gadget: A Manifesto*. New York: Vintage Books.

Laske, Otto. 1990. "The Computer as the Artist's Alter Ego." *Leonardo* 23:53–66.

Leary, James P. 1977. "White Guys' Stories of the Night Street." *Journal of the Folklore Institute* 14 (1/2): 59–71.

Legman, Gershon. (1968) 1982. *No Laughing Matter: An Analysis of Sexual Humor*. 2 vols. Bloomington: Indiana University Press.

Leppzer, Robert. 1980. *Voices from Three Mile Island: The People Speak Out*. Berkeley, CA: Crossing Press.

Levine, Lawrence W. 1988. *Highbrow/Lowbrow: The Emergence of Cultural Hierarchy in America*. Cambridge, MA: Harvard University Press.

Lewis, Paul. 2006. *Cracking Up: American Humor in a Time of Conflict*. Chicago: University of Chicago Press.

Lieber, Andrea. 2010. "Domesticity and the Home(Page): Blogging and the Blurring of Public and Private among Orthodox Jewish Women." In *Jews at Home: The Domestication of Identity*, edited by Simon J. Bronner, 258–82. Oxford, UK: Littman Library of Jewish Civilization.

Lifton, Robert Jay. 1968. *Death in Life: Survivors of Hiroshima*. New York: Random House.

———. 1969. *Boundaries: Psychological Man in Revolution*. New York: Simon and Schuster.

———. 1970. *History and Human Survival*. New York: Random House.

———. 1979. *The Broken Connection: On Death and the Continuity of Life*. New York: Simon and Schuster.

———. 1982. *Indefensible Weapons: The Political and Psychological Case Against Nuclearism*. New York: Basic Books.

Linke, Uli, and Alan Dundes. 1988. "More Auschwitz Jokes." *Folklore* 99 (1): 3–10.

Long, Sarah Ann. 2005. "Digital Natives: If You Aren't One, Get to Know One." *New Library World* 106 (3/4): 187–89.

Lovink, Geert. 2003. *Dark Fiber: Tracking Critical Internet Culture*. Cambridge, MA: MIT Press.

———. 2007. *Zero Comments: Blogging and Critical Internet Culture*. New York: Routledge.

Lowe, Donald M. 1983. *History of the Bourgeois Perception*. Chicago: University of Chicago Press.

Malmsheimer, Lonna M. 1986. "Three Mile Island: Fact, Frame, and Fiction." *American Quarterly* 38 (1): 35–52.

Marshall, P. David. 2006. *The Celebrity Culture Reader*. New York: Routledge.

Marx, Leo. 1964. *The Machine in the Garden: Technology and the Pastoral Ideal in America*. New York: Oxford University Press.

McCracken, Grant. 1988. *Culture and Consumption: New Approaches to the Symbolic Character of Consumer Goods and Activities*. Bloomington: Indiana University Press.

———. 1989. "'Homeyness': A Cultural Account of One Constellation of Consumer Goods and Meanings." In *Interpretive Consumer Research*, edited by Elizabeth C. Hirschman, 168–183. Provo, UT: Association for Consumer Research.

McDonald, Paul. 2001. *The Star System: Hollywood's Production of Popular Identities*. London: Wallflower Press.

McLuhan, Marshall. (1964) 1994. *Understanding Media: The Extensions of Man*. Cambridge, MA: MIT Press.

McLuhan, Marshall, and Quentin Fiore. (1967) 1989. *The Medium Is the Message*. New York: Touchstone.

McLure, Helen. 2000. "The Wild, Wild Web: The Mythic American West and the Electronic Frontier." *Western Historical Quarterly* 31:457–76.

McNeill, Lynne S. 2009. "The End of the Internet: A Folk Response to the Provision of Infinite Choice." In *Folklore and the Internet: Vernacular Expression in a Digital World*, edited by Trevor J. Blank, 80–97. Logan: Utah State University Press.

———. 2012. "Real Virtuality: Enhancing Locality by Enacting the Small World Theory." In *Folk Culture in the Digital Age: The Emergent Dynamics of Human Interaction*, edited by Trevor J. Blank, 85–97. Logan: Utah State University Press.

Mechling, Jay. 2002. "Children and Colors: Folk and Popular Cultures in America's Futures." In *Folk Nation: Folklore in the Creation of American Tradition*, edited by Simon J. Bronner, 263–83. Wilmington, DE: Scholarly Resources Books.

———. 2006. "Solo Folklore." *Western Folklore* 65:435–54.

Michael, Nancy. 1995. "Censure of a Photocopylore Display." *Journal of Folklore Research* 32 (2): 137–54.

Michaelis, Vicki. 2003. "Bryant Trial Will Be 'Ugly.'" *USA Today*, July 20. http://tinyurl.com/KobeTrial. Accessed August 9, 2011.

Miller, Kiri. 2008. "Grove Street Grimm: Grand Theft Auto and Digital Folklore." *Journal of American Folklore* 121 (481): 255–85.

Milspaw, Yvonne J. 1981. "Folklore and the Nuclear Age: 'The Harrisburg Disaster' at Three Mile Island." *International Review of Folklore* 1:57–65.

———. 2007. "TMI-2: Elements in the Discourse of Disaster." *Contemporary Legend*, new series 10:74–93.

Mitchell, Roger. 1979. "The Press, Rumor, and Legend Formation." *Midwestern Journal of Language and Lore* 5:1–2.

Moore, Robert J., E. Cabell Hankinson Gathman, and Nicolas Ducheneau. 2009. "From 3D Space to Third Place: The Social Life of Small Virtual Spaces." *Human Organization* 68 (2): 230–40.

Morozov, Evan. 2011. *The Net Delusion: The Dark Side of Internet Freedom*. New York: PublicAffairs Books.

Morreall, John. 1983. *Taking Laughter Seriously*. Albany: State University of New York Press.

Narváez, Peter, ed. 2003. *Of Corpse: Death and Humor in Folklore and Popular Culture*. Logan: Utah State University Press.

National Enquirer. 2009. "World Exclusive: Woman at Center of Tiger Woods Cheating Scandal Exposed." *National Enquirer*, November 28. http://www.national enquirer.com/celebrity/67747. Accessed September 16, 2010.

Newell, William Wells. 1883. *Games and Songs of American Children*. New York: Harper.

Nimmo, Dan, and James E. Combs. 1985. *Nightly Horrors: Crisis Coverage in Television Network News*. Knoxville: University of Tennessee Press.

O'Reilly, Tim. 2005. "What Is Web 2.0? Design Patterns and Business Models for the Next Generation of Software." *O'Reilly Media*, September 30. http://oreilly.com /web2/archive/what-is-web-20.html. Accessed August 3, 2011.

Oring, Elliott. 1976. "Three Functions of Folklore: Traditional Functionalism as Explanation in Folkloristics." *Journal of American Folklore* 89:67–80.

———. 1983. "The People of the Joke: On the Conceptualization of a Jewish Humor." *Western Folklore* 42 (4): 261–71.

———. 1984a. "Dyadic Traditions." *Journal of Folklore Research* 21 (1): 19–28.

———. 1984b. "Jokes and Their Relation to Sigmund Freud." *Western Folklore* 43 (1): 37–48.

———. 1987. "Jokes and the Discourse on Disaster." *Journal of American Folklore* 100 (397): 276–86.

———. 1992. *Jokes and Their Relations*. Lexington: University Press of Kentucky.

———. 1995. "Arbiters of Taste: An Afterword." *Journal of Folklore Research* 32 (2): 165–74.

———. 2003. *Engaging Humor*. Urbana: University of Illinois Press.

Ornstein, Severo. 2002. *Computing in the Middle Ages: A View from the Trenches, 1955–1983*. Bloomington, IN: AuthorHouse.

Osif, Bonnie A. 2004. *TMI 25 Years Later: The Three Mile Island Nuclear Power Plant Accident and Its Impact*. University Park: Pennsylvania State University Press.

Palvrey, John, and Urs Gasser. 2008. *Born Digital: Understanding the First Generation of Digital Natives*. New York: Basic Books.

Peceny, Mark. 1997. "A Constructivist Interpretation of the Liberal Peace: The Ambiguous Case of the Spanish-American War." *Journal of Peace Research* 34 (4): 415–30.

Plasketes, George. 1999. "Things to Do in Littleton When You're Dead: A Post Columbine Collage." *Popular Music and Society* 23 (3): 9–24.

Plato. 1992. *Republic*. Edited by C. D. C. Reeve. Translated by G. M. A. Grube. Indianapolis: Hackett.

Pope, Mark, and Matt Englar-Carlson. 2001. "Fathers and Sons: The Relationship Between Violence and Masculinity." *The Family Journal* 9 (4): 367–74.

Prensky, Marc. 2001a. "Digital Natives, Digital Immigrants." *On the Horizon* 9 (5): 1–6.

———. 2001b. "Digital Natives, Digital Immigrants, Part II: Do They Really *Think* Differently?" *On the Horizon* 9 (6): 1–6.

———. 2004. "The Emerging Online Life of the Digital Native: What They Do Differently Because of Technology, and How They Do It." Unpublished manuscript.

———. 2006. *Don't Bother Me, Mom—I'm Learning!* St. Paul, MN: Paragon House.

———. 2007. *Digital Game-Based Learning*. St. Paul, MN: Paragon House.

Preston, Michael J. 1974. "Xerox-lore." *Keystone Folklore Quarterly* 19:11–26.

———. 1994. "Traditional Humor from the Fax Machine: 'All of a Kind.'" *Western Folklore* 53 (2): 147–69.

Provine, Robert R. 2000. *Laughter: A Scientific Investigation*. New York: Penguin.

Putnam, Robert D. 1995. "Bowling Alone: America's Declining Social Capital." *Journal of Democracy* 6 (1): 65–78.

———. 2000. *Bowling Alone: The Collapse and Revival of American Community*. New York: Simon and Schuster.

Rasmussen, Scott, and Doug Schoen. 2010. *Mad as Hell: How the Tea Party Movement Is Fundamentally Remaking Our Two-Party System*. New York: Harper.

Rawlinson, Linnie, and Nick Hunt. 2009. "Jackson Dies, Almost Takes Internet with Him." CNN, June 26. http://www.cnn.com/2009/TECH/06/26/michael.jackson.internet/index.html. Accessed October 31, 2009.

Rec.Humor.Funny Newsgroup Archives. 1999. "Priceless." April. http://www.netfunny.com/rhf/jokes/99/Apr/columbine.html. Accessed August 12, 2011.

Redfield, Robert. 1947. "The Folk Society." *American Journal of Sociology* 52 (4): 293–308.

Rheingold, Howard. 2000. *The Virtual Community: Homesteading on the Electronic Frontier*. Cambridge, MA: MIT Press.

———. 2003. *Smart Mobs: The Next Social Generation*. New York: Basic Books.

Richtel, Matt. 2010. "Growing Up Digital, Wired for Distraction." *New York Times*, November 21. http://tinyurl.com/NYTWiredForDistraction. Accessed November 21, 2010.

Riesman, David (with Nathan Glazer and Reuel Denney). (1950) 1961. *The Lonely Crowd: A Study of the Changing American Character*. New Haven, CT: Yale University Press.

Roemer, Danielle M. 1994. "Photocopy Lore and the Naturalization of the Corporate Body." *Journal of American Folklore* 107 (423): 121–38.

Romanoff, Bronna D., and Marion Terenzio. 1998. "Rituals and the Grieving Process." *Death Studies* 22 (8): 697–711.

Rosenberg, Scott. 2009. *Say Everything: How Blogging Began, What It's Becoming, and Why It Matters*. New York: Crown.

Ryan, Johnny. 2010. *A History of the Internet and the Digital Future*. London: Reaktion Books.

Samuelson, Sue. 1995. "A Review of the Distinctive Genres of Adolescent Folklore." *Children's Folklore Review* 17:13–32.

Santino, Jack. 1995. *All Around the Year: Holidays and Celebrations in American Life*. Urbana: University of Illinois Press.

———. 2005. *Spontaneous Shrines and Public Memorialization of Death*. New York: Palgrave MacMillan.

Schickel, Richard. 1985. *Intimate Strangers: The Cult of Celebrity*. Chicago: Ivan R. Dee.

Shirky, Clay. 2008. *Here Comes Everybody: The Power of Organizing Without Organizations*. New York: Penguin.

———. 2010. *Cognitive Surplus: Creativity and Generosity in a Connected Age*. New York: Penguin.

Simons, Elizabeth Radin. 1986. "The NASA Joke Cycle: The Astronauts and the Teachers." *Western Folklore* 45 (4): 261–77.

Singer, Eleanor, and Phyllis M. Endreny. 1993. *Reporting on Risk: How the Mass Media Portray Accidents, Diseases, Disasters, and Other Hazards*. New York: Russell Sage Foundation.

Smith, Moira. 1990. "Jokes and Practical Jokes." In *The Emergence of Folklore in Everyday Life*, edited by George H. Schoemaker, 73–82. Bloomington, IN: Trickster Press.

Smith, Paul. 1991. "The Joke Machine: Communicating Traditional Humour Using Computers." In *Spoken In Jest*, edited by Gillian Bennett, 257–77. Sheffield, UK: Sheffield Academic Press.

Smyth, Willie. 1986. "Challenger Jokes and the Humor of Disaster." *Western Folklore* 45 (4): 243–60.

Sofka, Carla J. 2009. "News and Notes: Adventures of a Thanatologist: The Cultural Reincarnation of Michael Jackson." *Death Studies* 33 (10): 958–60.

Spigel, Lynn. 1991. "Communicating with the Dead: Elvis as Medium." *Camera Obscura* 23:176–205.

Stallabrass, Julian. 2003. *Internet Art: The Online Clash of Culture and Commerce*. Mustang, OK: Tate.

Stross, Brian. 1999. "The Hybrid Metaphor: From Biology to Culture." *Journal of American Folklore* 112 (445): 254–67.

Susman, Warren. 1984. *Culture as History: The Transformation of American Society in the Twentieth Century*. New York: Pantheon Books.

Tapscott, Dan. 1999. *Growing Up Digital: The Rise of the Net Generation*. New York: McGraw-Hill.

———. 2008. *Grown Up Digital: How the Net Generation Is Changing Your World*. New York: McGraw-Hill.

Thomas, Jeannie Banks. 1997. "Dumb Blondes, Dan Quayle, and Hillary Clinton: Gender, Sexuality, and Stupidity in Jokes." *Journal of American Folklore* 110 (437): 277–31.

Thompson, Krissah. 2009. "Harvard Scholar Henry Louis Gates Arrested." *Washington Post*, July 21. http://tinyurl.com/HLGates2009. Accessed October 1, 2010.

Tithecott, Richard. 1997. *Of Men and Monsters: Jeffrey Dahmer and the Construction of the Serial Killer.* Madison: University of Wisconsin Press.

Trachtenberg, Alan. (1982) 2007. *The Incorporation of America: Culture and Society in the Gilded Age.* New York: Hill and Wang.

Turkle, Sherry. 1995. *Life on the Screen: Identity in the Age of the Internet.* New York: Simon and Schuster.

———. 2005. *The Second Self: Computers and the Human Spirit.* Cambridge, MA: MIT Press.

———. 2011. *Alone Together: Why We Expect More from Technology and Less from Each Other.* New York: Basic Books.

Turner, Fred. 2008. *From Counterculture to Cyberculture: Stewart Brand, the Whole Earth Network, and the Rise of Digital Utopianism.* Chicago: University of Chicago Press.

Turner, Frederick Jackson. 1893. "The Significance of the Frontier in American History." *Proceedings of the State Historical Society of Wisconsin*, December 14. http://xroads.virginia.edu/~hyper/turner/chapter1.html. Accessed October 5, 2010.

———. 1961. *Frontier and Section: Selected Essays of Frederick Jackson Turner.* Englewood Cliffs, NJ: Prentice-Hall.

Turner, Viktor. 1974. "Liminal to Liminoid in Play, Flow, and Ritual: An Essay in Comparative Symbology." *Rice University Studies* 60 (3): 53–92.

Untiedt, Kenneth, ed. 2006. *Folklore: In All of Us, In All We Do.* Publications of the Texas Folklore Society 63. Denton: University of North Texas Press.

Van Grove, Jennifer. 2010. "United States Internet Speed Is on the Decline." *Mashable*, January 16. http://mashable.com/2010/01/16/united-states-internet-speed/. Accessed August 3, 2011.

Vickio, Craig J. 1999. "Together in Spirit: Keeping Our Relationships Alive When Loved Ones Die." *Death Studies* 23 (2): 161–75.

Vygotsky, Lev. 1978. *Mind in Society.* Cambridge, MA: Harvard University Press.

Walker, J. Samuel. 2006. *Three Mile Island: A Nuclear Crisis in Historical Perspective.* Berkeley: University of California Press.

Warnick, Barbara. 2007. *Rhetoric Online: Persuasion and Politics on the World Wide Web.* New York: Peter Lang.

Weber, Sandra, and Shanly Dixon. 2007. *Growing Up Online: Young People and Digital Technologies.* New York: Palgrave Macmillan.

Wehmeyer, Stephen C., and Kerry Noonan. 2009. "Re-envisioning the Visionary: Towards a Behavior Definition of Initiatory Art." *Western Folklore* 67 (2/3): 199–222.

Weiss, Aaron. 2006. "The Last Word: The Ugly Web—Where Form Follows Way Behind Function." *netWorker* 10 (2): 40–43.

Wenger, Dennis E., James D. Dykes, Thomas D. Sebok, and Joan L. Neff. 1975. "It's a Matter of Myths: An Empirical Examination of Individual Insight into Disaster Response." *Mass Emergencies* 1:33–46.

Wenger, Dennis E., and Barbara Friedman. 1986. *Local and National Media Coverage of Disasters: A Content Analysis of the Print Media's Treatment of Disaster Myths.* Newark: Disaster Research Center, University of Delaware.

Westerman, William. 2009. "Epistemology, the Sociology of Knowledge, and the *Wikipedia* Userbox Controversy." In *Folklore and the Internet: Vernacular Expression in a Digital World,* edited by Trevor J. Blank, 123–58. Logan: Utah State University Press.

Whyte, Kenneth. 2009. *The Uncrowned King: The Sensationalist Rise of William Randolph Hearst.* Berkeley, CA: Counterpoint Press.

Wilden, Anthony. 1980. *System and Structure: Essays in Communication and Exchange.* 2nd ed. London: Tavistock.

Wojcik, Daniel. 2009. "Outsider Art, Vernacular Traditions, Trauma, and Creativity." *Western Folklore* 67 (2/3): 179–98.

Wolfenstein, Martha, and Gilbert Kliman. 1965. *Children and the Death of a President.* Garden City, NJ: Doubleday Books.

Wright, John C., Dale Kunkel, Marites Pinon, and Aletha C. Huston. 1989. "How Children Reacted to Televised Coverage of the Space Shuttle Disaster." *Journal of Communication* 39 (2): 27–45.

Wuthnow, Robert. 2010. *Be Very Afraid: The Cultural Response to Terror, Pandemics, Environmental Devastation, Nuclear Annihilation, and Other Threats.* New York: Oxford University Press.

Yarbrough, Tyrone. 1998. "Consider the Source: Conspiracy Theories, Narratives, and Belief." *New Directions in Folklore* 2. https://scholarworks.iu.edu/dspace/handle/2022/3876.

Zukin, Sharon. 2005. *Point of Purchase: How Shopping Changed American Culture.* New York: Routledge.

Index

FOLKLORE STUDIES
IN A MULTICULTURAL
WORLD

*The Last Laugh: Folk Humor, Celebrity Culture, and Mass-Mediated
Disasters in the Digital Age* (University of Wisconsin Press)
TREVOR J. BLANK

Squeeze This! A Cultural History of the Accordion in America
(University of Illinois Press)
MARION JACOBSON

*The Jumbies' Playing Ground: Old World Influences on Afro-Creole
Masquerades in the Eastern Caribbean* (University Press of Mississippi)
ROBERT WYNDHAM NICHOLLS